Praise for *The Absurdity of Compromise*

Author Don Grady has helped resolve seemingly intractable conflicts around the world, including in Bosnia-Herzegovina during the 1990s as well as in cities, businesses, and universities throughout the U.S. Now he offers a fresh perspective on conflict resolution based on these real-life experiences.

Today's practices often present antagonists with one-sided solutions, leaving each feeling like losers. In Grady's peace-building schemata, everyone comes away a winner. He uses the Socratic method to bring out the best in his protagonists, showing us how to build win-win outcomes in the complex and evolving field of conflict resolution.

I recommend this lively book to anyone enmeshed in a conflict needing a resolution, foreign or domestic.

Robert W. Farrand,

U.S. Ambassador (Retired)

Deputy High Representative, Bosnia-Herzegovina, 1997-2000

THE
ABSURDITY
OF
COMPROMISE

The Art of Resolving Conflict so Everyone Wins

Donald Grady II, PhD

HUGO HOUSE PUBLISHERS

Cover Design & Interior Layout: Yolanda Ciolli

ISBN 978-1-948261-14-2 Paperback
ISBN 978-1-948261-15-9 Hardback

Library of Congress Control Number: 2018960324

Hugo House Publishers
Denver, Colorado
Austin, Texas
www.HugoHousePublishers.com

Dedicated To:

The Magnificent Men of 2519

ɔom ´prō·mīse (Oxford English Dictionary)

[noun]

    1 *An agreement or settlement of a dispute that is reached by each side making concessions.*
    1.1 *An intermediate state between conflicting alternatives reached by mutual concession.*
    2 *The expedient acceptance of standards that are lower than is desirable.*

[verb]

    1 *Settle a dispute by mutual concession.*
    2 *Expediently accept standards that are lower than is desirable.*
    2.1 *Weaken or harm by accepting standards that are lower than is desirable.*

[verb-with object]

    3 *Bring into disrepute or danger by indiscreet, foolish, or reckless behavior.*
    3.1 *Cause to become vulnerable or function less effectively.*

Table of Contents

Introduction

All our lives we've been told that to get something you must give something. That sentiment is as pervasive today as ever. You can find it in almost every aspect of life, from political wrangling, to world leaders trading aid for disarmament, to parents negotiating with children over vegetables and dessert.

People like to point to compromise as "the way" to get things done—but rarely does anyone leave excited about the outcome. Have you ever compromised, but didn't feel particularly satisfied with the way it ended?

Why compromise if the result is likely to make you and everyone else unhappy? I've never understood the rationale behind this thinking. It's a conflicted notion. Compromise too often leads to resentment, which most people would prefer to avoid.

I've traveled the world over, fostering change in some of the most challenging environments imaginable, including war zones where life and death were at stake. Most disagreements aren't likely to result in attempts at mutual destruction. That said, you are likely to have a few disagreements in your lifetime. Most will be fairly benign, but some could turn hostile, perhaps even violent.

The concepts introduced in these pages are a product of my personal experiences working alongside some of the most talented people on the planet. Figuratively speaking, I've been tasked with doing "the impossible" with "nothing," and one of the most important lessons I've learned is that the impossible often isn't.

However, if compromise is your method of choice, then the impossible is far more probable. What I mean is that when you compromise you necessarily surrender something. You inevitably wind up taking part of the dispute away with you as a loss. Doing the impossible is winning, but you can't win if you've already lost.

If you look for common ground and use your common sense, you'll open the door to winning. There are very important differences between the terms "compromise" and "common ground." They are *not* the same, and we'll wrestle with the differences in some detail later.

The characters presented here are reflective of people we've all dealt with. You already know them. You've likely spent time alongside or across the table from them at some point in your life. My hope is that the levels of personal interaction presented through their allegory will allow you to turn a mirror on yourself and see where and how you can apply the tools provided in this work to your advantage.

You'll need to look behind the curtain. Look "compromise" in the face and see it for what it really is. Your principles and values give credence to who you are. They define you. Your willingness to compromise them— even something seemingly insignificant—diminishes your character. You're not alone. Everybody does it. Day after day we find ourselves adjusting to the world, compromising for the sake of getting along. You learned long ago that repeating a behavior while expecting a different outcome is foolhardy at best. Well…

It's time to break the cycle. It is time to stop compromising and start winning.

What's Wrong with This Picture?

It rained the night before. A wall of swollen and dingy looking clouds hung low in the sky, casting a stifling pall on everything below. The air was hot and dank. The plants seemed fatigued in the still air. They drooped limply for the lack of a breeze.

How fitting, Sage thought. She felt a bit droopy and not overly energetic herself.

She slowed her pace, perhaps to stay in sync with her melancholy. Sage had been helping people find ways to compromise her entire life. Even as a child she'd played the mediator. She usually felt good about it, but last week she'd run into a former client. She was dumbfounded when he began grousing about a mediation she'd facilitated between him and another company months ago.

He'd rudely pointed his finger at her face and shouted he should never have accepted the terms of that stupid agreement. Sage reminded him that no one ever gets everything they want in a compromise. "I'm sick of people telling me that," he said. Then he abruptly huffed off, muttering to himself.

Sage's colleagues continually reinforced the idea that the best solutions were often the result of compromises. "Everybody gets something," they'd say. "It's a win/win." But since her encounter of the previous week, Sage couldn't shake the feeling that something just wasn't quite right with that line of reasoning. Now that she thought about it, whenever she'd brokered a supposedly "successful" compromise, everyone involved left more-or-less dissatisfied. In fact, Sage reflected, she hadn't been completely satisfied either.

So, what's wrong with this picture?

"Damn this weather!" she said out loud to herself, since no one else was close enough to hear. The sun had been playing a game of peek-a-boo but was now simply hiding, heightening her sense of gloom.

Sage was a facilitator by profession, and she'd mediated some of the most difficult contracts and settled some of the most contentious disputes her firm had ever faced. She could get people to compromise when the other partners couldn't get them to budge. Normally, Sage was proud of that, but today she was having a difficult time wrapping her head around the value of it.

Sage thought about how much she liked winning. Winning produced accolades and lots of money, but now she felt as if she'd been fooling herself all along. Thinking back to when she'd orchestrated a "really good" compromise in the past, she hadn't really been all that excited about it. Today that was troubling her. In retrospect, nobody who'd been involved in her previous interventions had been overly taken with the results. People were generally happy when the process ended, but they weren't particularly happy with the *outcomes*. Sighing, Sage thought, *And there I was patting myself on the back for making everyone unhappy.* She shook her head, but she couldn't shake the feeling that something was very wrong with what she'd been doing.

To clear her mind, Sage had gone for an early morning run, but ended up more conflicted than when she'd started. She took a deep breath, drawing morning air deep into her lungs. It burned her throat and made her cough. *Okay, time for something new.* Sage decided her best course of action was to find a way to settle disagreements without those unhappy outcomes—if that was even possible. Throughout her career Sage had watched people turn minor mediations into uncomfortable settlements. Worse yet, she'd seen some turn into destructive "I win/you lose", zero-sum confrontations. As she thought about it, Sage realized she had occasionally done that as well.

I'm going to make it my mission to learn how to resolve conflict without making the clients feel as though they've lost something they'd rather have kept, Sage mused to herself.

To her credit, Sage embarked on a comprehensive study of the subject. She decided that if she was going to learn something, she needed to let go of the idea that she "already knew" everything. But university courses, management classes, and business seminars turned out to be fruitless undertakings. Sage found nothing in these endeavors to help. The search was taking forever, and she was no closer to improving her outcomes than when she'd started.

Sage started attending mediations conducted by some of the most renowned facilitators in the country. She encountered negotiators of every ilk. Some completely dominated the discussion. Others routinely got both parties to sacrifice something important, hoping for something in return. "That's the way the world works," they'd say. "You gotta give something to get something." But for all their giving and getting, those involved too often left unhappy. If she'd heard it once she'd heard it a hundred times: "You know you've brokered a good deal when everyone leaves unhappy." Disillusioned, Sage pondered, *Is that it? Is this all there is?*

Down, but not out, she resolved to keep searching. Then a friend told her about a woman he'd met at a union negotiation who'd seemed to work wonders. He said

Human Resource Services, the department he worked for, was currently involved in a tough negotiation with the same facilitator. He offered to wrangle an invitation for Sage to attend as an observer. She accepted without hesitation.

2

Listen to What You're Hearing

Sage was having a crazy day. She'd gotten caught in a traffic jam. As a result, she was more than two hours late for the session her friend had arranged for her to observe. When she finally arrived, she grabbed a seat and prepared for what she anticipated would be another lengthy day of disagreements. But then the most peculiar thing happened. Before she could settle in, the meeting was over. Everyone rose from their seats and left the room smiling, shaking hands, and genuinely congratulating each other. A man on his way out glanced her way, so she quickly stopped him. "Excuse me," she said, looking confused, "But what just happened?"

The man smiled, motioned with his thumb over his right shoulder at a woman in the room gathering her papers, and said, "She happened." Then he turned and continued down the corridor.

Sage decided to wait until the woman finished collecting her things before she approached. "I was supposed to observe today," Sage explained, "but I'm afraid I was too late. I obviously missed something important."

The woman smiled. "There'll be other opportunities," she said.

"I thought this was supposed to be a difficult mediation."

"It was," the woman replied.

"Then I don't understand," Sage said, her confusion evident. "You weren't in here long enough to have finished a session as difficult as this one was purported to be."

Smiling benevolently, the woman responded. "Difficult doesn't always mean it'll take a long time." She hefted her bag onto her shoulder, extended her hand and said, "You are?"

Sage took the woman's hand. "My friends call me Sage."

"Pleased to meet you, Sage. Everyone calls me MJ," the woman said warmly as she shook Sage's hand. Then she turned, left the room and started down the hallway.

Sage followed, quickening her pace so she could catch up to the other woman. "How were you able to get them to compromise so quickly?" she asked.

The woman slowed so she could look Sage in the eye. "Compromise?" she asked. "No one compromised. They got what they needed to satisfy their interest."

"No way," Sage said, half under her breath.

MJ studied Sage for a moment, deciding whether to pursue the matter. Then, she raised an eyebrow in a friendly fashion, nodded her head with a smile, and simply said, "Yes, way."

"Is that even *possible*?" Sage asked, shaking her head and frowning.

"Apparently it is," MJ replied, still smiling. And with that, she again walked away. Sage stood there for a moment, befuddled. Then she walked to her car while pondering the interaction and then got on with the rest of her day.

* * * * *

Sage couldn't get the woman out of her head. She desperately wanted to learn the key to what had looked like a stress-free mediation. So a few days later, she looked up the number for the agency MJ worked for and placed a call. The only name the woman had given Sage was MJ. She felt odd calling the woman's office and asking for "MJ." However, the person who answered the phone immediately knew who she was asking for and called the woman MJ herself. That made Sage feel a little better, but not entirely. MJ's assistant arranged a meeting for Sage at MJ's office the following week.

Sage arrived as scheduled. The office was spacious and well-appointed. Sage was admiring the room's lack of pretense when MJ offered her a refreshment and asked, "How can I help you?"

Sage declined the drink. "I don't want to take a lot of your time," she said as she settled into the chair MJ indicated. "The reason I'm here is that I would really like to know how you managed to get an agreement without someone leaving unhappy. As I'd understood it, beforehand they were vehemently opposed to a settlement of any kind."

MJ smiled graciously. "That's what you asked me about the other day, wasn't it?"

Sage nodded. "Yes—I mean, is it even possible to get a person to sacrifice something they care about without being dissatisfied when it's all over?"

MJ chuckled. "You think I got those people to make sacrifices. And you want to know how I did it?

"Well, yes," Sage answered, nodding sheepishly. "I want to be able to get those kinds of results too, but for the life of me, I haven't been able to figure out how. But it seems you have."

"Perhaps," MJ said, her face giving nothing away. "You want the secret to making people happy while getting them to sacrifice? Do I have that right?" She paused but Sage didn't answer.

MJ continued after waiting a few moments. "If that's what you're here for, you've come to the wrong place."

"Oh," Sage said, surprised. "But I thought..." Then she trailed off.

MJ chuckled. "I didn't mean to put you on the spot."

Sage smiled back, grateful for the reprieve. "I do this

stuff for a living too," She said. "But after years of getting people to sacrifice for the sake of agreement, it doesn't make sense to me anymore. I'm tired of getting the "good compromise" only to find that nobody is happy with the outcome. But what I saw the other day, I'd give gobs of good money for that secret."

MJ smiled a little harder. Unthinkingly, she folded her hands in her lap while gently rubbing her thumbs together. "I don't have any secrets," she said, "and I don't make people happy for sacrificing or for giving stuff up they'd rather keep. I don't know anyone who *can*."

"But," Sage said, "the people from the meeting the other day—they *were* happy as they left." She paused for a moment, remembering. "I saw it. How did you get to that point?"

MJ leaned forward. "It's all in the way you approach it. It's not what you say or how you say it. It's how well you *understand* someone else's perspectives and how you communicate that understanding back to them." She gestured around the room as if indicating other people were listening in. "It's in how you open the door to the legitimate feelings and expressions of others. It's in your willingness to accept and to empathize with those holding differing positions."

"Okay, I know what I think empathy is," Sage said. "But that word is not always interpreted the same by everyone who uses it. So, tell me what does empathize mean to *you*."

"Let's see how it's defined online first," MJ suggested. "Okay, here it is." While reading from her phone she said, "Wikipedia defines empathy as '...the capacity to understand or feel what another person is experiencing from within their frame of reference, i.e., the capacity to place oneself in another's position.' Is that how you'd define it?"

"Pretty much," Sage replied. "That's not a bad explanation."

"I agree," MJ said. "But from my perspective empathy goes deeper than the Wikipedia definition I just read suggests. I see it more as developing an intimate understanding of someone else's experiences." MJ used air quotes to emphasize the word, *intimate*. "It's sensing the depth and breadth of somebody else's emotions, their feelings, their pain, sorrow, joy, fear, and anxieties. You must internalize their reality as if it were your own. See it as if you were looking at it with their eyes. Feel it as if you were touching it with their hands. Intuit it with the intensity of their emotions. You should ask yourself how you'd feel if you were living in their skin. It's not feeling sorry for someone. It's as close as you can get to being that someone.

MJ looked more closely at Sage and asked, "Does that make sense?"

"Perfect," Sage answered. "It makes perfect sense. In fact, I think I like your definition better."

"Good," MJ said before continuing. "Once you understand empathetically what the other person feels, then you must assist *them* in understanding *why* they hold the position they've taken."

Sage was nodding, but also frowning a little at the same time. MJ noticed and hesitated for a moment before continuing. "This is really important. Nothing I've just told you matters if you don't realize and accept as fact that it's not about you. Never has been. Never will be. It's about doing with and for others what you know to be good and right. Do that, and you'll always win."

The frown Sage was wearing disappeared and her face seemed to brighten a little. "Winning!" Sage said, "That's what I'm talking about!" But, as if remembering something oppressive, she sank back into her chair, frowning again and appearing somewhat deflated. "I thought I and everyone else was winning when I'd get to a compromise," she said. "But it...never felt right." Then a hint of a smile broke at the corner of Sage's mouth. "If I can make things happen like what I saw you do the other day, I'll be winning again. For real this time."

"You got there after it was all over, so I'm afraid you didn't see very much," MJ said.

"Well, I didn't see what got them there, but I saw the results," Sage said. "And in all my years, I've never seen anyone get results like that."

"In the past you probably witnessed other facilitators use bullying tactics to get what they wanted and perhaps even adopted some of those same techniques for yourself," MJ said, pausing momentarily for confirmation.

Sage nodded lamentably and said, "You're not wrong." Then she pinched her lips together so tightly they looked more like a slit below her nose than a mouth.

"Bullying and compromise do not make for happy reconciliations," MJ said. "In fact, those tactics will likely result in some very unhappy customers." She paused again. Sage thought back and then bobbed her head up and down as she remembered her encounter with the guy in the mall.

MJ continued, "You want to know how to achieve outcomes like the one you witnessed the other day? You start by listening."

"Listening?" Sage asked incredulously.

MJ nodded. "Yes, listening," she said crossing her legs and reclining in her chair.

Sage looked up. "Don't stop," she said. "I'm on pins and needles here."

That made MJ smile.

"Okay," MJ said. She tilted her head, as if to say *You ready for this?* "I'm about to share some things with you that if you take them to heart, are likely to make a profound difference in your professional and personal life."

"Shoot," Sage said, rocking forward in anticipation. "That's exactly why I came."

"Well, all right then," MJ began. "There are plenty of books, manuscripts, and all kinds of online data available for you to digest. There's so much it's almost impossible to keep up with the latest, greatest techniques and tactics about negotiation. The ability to communicate and manage effectively is the stuff success is made of. The art of good management is in how you communicate. That's what we do as facilitators."

Sage was a little anxious. "I know how to communicate," she said. "It's what I do."

"Do you?" MJ asked. "Didn't you tell me just a little while ago that you aren't happy with the results you've been achieving?"

"I did," said Sage. "But how to communicate? Really? I can get a point across and influence people to get things done better than most people. I take pride in that."

MJ looked at her a moment. "Communication is more than just talking, you know? You need to listen, too. I mean really listen. Additionally, you need to have patience. That's how you get the positive outcomes you say you want."

That made Sage scooch back in her chair a bit. She'd been told a thousand times that she needed to have more patience. But she was tired of *being patient*. She wanted answers. She'd been looking for what seemed like forever, and she was ready to be finished with it.

"Okay," Sage said resignedly. "I'm big enough to admit that I haven't gotten even close to the results you obtained the other day. I have some learning to do. So, go ahead, I'm listening."

MJ knew Sage was frustrated, but that wasn't necessarily a bad thing. Sage was facing something she now realized had been confounding her efforts and best intentions throughout her career.

MJ continued in a calmer and more even tone. "What I mean by 'listen' is to listen with every part of your being, not just your ears. Be prepared to reconcile what you've heard with what *you* know to be true and right. And then help the other person analyze their position and to reframe it as necessary so they satisfy their interests. One of the most important aspects of being a good facilitator is understanding the underlying philosophy or ideology that guides *your own* thinking and your ability to synthesize new information appropriately and effectively with others."

Sage opened her mouth to speak, but MJ held up a hand, anticipating her protest. "No," she said, "I'm not about to give you another *Seven Habits* or point you in the direction of a *One Minute* guru. That's already been done." She gestured in a sweeping motion. "The world is full of people who believe that they're 'principled' and who strive for 'excellence,'" she said, making air quotes. "Don't get me wrong. I love *The One Minute Manager* and *The Seven Habits of Highly Successful People*. I work hard to achieve excellence in everything I do, but it's not enough to know what to do and how to do it. You'll need to be intensely committed. Others will gravitate to you if they can see and feel how intensely you care about them and that you love who you are and what you do." MJ leaned forward with a big grin on her face. "There, I said it—the 'L' word." She smiled as she observed Sage's reaction.

3

What's Love Got to Do with It?

Sage was dumbfounded, and it showed. "You're kidding, right?"

Still smiling, MJ shook her head. "Nope," she said, "I'm not." She wiped several strands of her shoulder-length auburn hair out of her eyes. "The best facilitators I know are committed 'lovers.' They love who they are. They love what they do, and they're very particular about how they get it done."

"I've not heard that before," Sage said. "Wasn't in the curriculum at law school."

"No. They don't teach this stuff in law school—I know I didn't get it." MJ replied. "That might be part of the problem. Too few people really love what they do. It's just a job. But the best entrepreneurs, farmers, police officers, teachers, nurses, facilitators...you name it, are all intensely committed. They don't merely *do* a thing. They feel it, and they let it show as they interact with others. You need zest and passion for what you do. And you've got to communicate it in a way that demonstrates your commitment."

"It's getting a tad warm in here, don't you think? I'm gonna get something to drink. You want anything?" MJ offered.

"I'll take you up on that," Sage accepted. "I'm getting a little thirsty myself."

MJ got a bottle of water for each of them and sat back down. She took a lingering drink then picked up right where she'd left off.

"It doesn't matter whether you're negotiating for your own interests," she said, "tending to personal affairs, or if you're working on behalf of a CEO of an international conglomerate. You have an obligation to know what's important to succeed. And the truly important things in life are usually much bigger than a handful of accepted management imperatives, the Dow Jones, or the Hang Seng indices."

"Yeah, but this is business we're talking..." Sage began, before trailing off.

MJ smiled. "In business, like everything else, it's not enough to merely say the right things. And the arena you're working in doesn't matter either. More than understanding what to do or how to do it, honest to God, you've got to put some *love into it*."

Sage was quiet for a moment, letting MJ's words turn over in her mind.

"This is what I mean," MJ offered. "The idea of love in the workplace is a foreign concept. It's an issue we face every day though. You see, love is not merely some romantic affection one feels for another. Although, that is pretty special," she said. "No, love is the intense feeling of attachment or commitment to something. It's unconditional, it's giving and forgiving. Love is power: it drives us and gives us strength in times of crisis or weakness. What you and I do requires us to lead. Leading is like parenting. Some mothers and fathers are terrible parents. Nevertheless, they are parents. Likewise, not everyone who purports to lead is good at it. But just because they're not good at it doesn't mean they are not doing it."

"I do love what I do," Sage said in retort. "I just don't like the way I feel about the outcomes I get or the way my clients feel about what I do sometimes. But I love what I do."

"I'm sure you do," MJ replied. "You want to be better. In fact, *you* want to be the best. Because you love it. Leading is integral to our successes in business, your family, the country, religion, politics and practically any other undertaking you can think of. So, basically, I'm saying you have to love to lead. I mean that in the sense of having a zeal for life and an intense commitment to others while at the same time relishing the activity itself."

"Do you have children?" MJ asked, seemingly out of nowhere.

Sage was startled by the abrupt change of the topic. "I have a three-year-old son," she said. "He's a handful but…!" Sage smiled, recalling her son's penchant for getting into mischief. "Why?"

"You love him?" MJ asked.

"Of course I do."

"Tell me what that looks like. What does loving your son look like?"

Sage paused to think. "It's like, you know…." She tried to find a way to put her thoughts into words. Stuttering slightly, she said, "It's like getting everything you could possibly want—and a piece of cake." She paused momentarily, smiling. "I love just holding him. The way he smells and giggles when I tickle him. I love watching him play with his father and the way the two of them look when they've fallen asleep together watching *Paddy the Alligator*. Or when he tells me it's 'peanut butter jelly time.'"

"Thank you. That was really good. Now think about what you just said," MJ asked. "You just told me that he makes you happy pretty much all of the time. What are you willing to give for that?"

Sage thought. "Everything. I am willing to give just about anything in the world to hold on to that."

"Okay," MJ said. "Now tell me how you feel about your job? Do you love being at work all day? Do you love being able to interact with everybody else at the office, getting a cup of coffee, or just standing at the water cooler?"

"Not exactly," Sage said.

"No?" MJ asked. "No urge to sing? Work is your life. You spend more of your waking hours at work than anywhere else. You spend more time interacting with clients and colleagues than with your family. So let me ask you this: Could some of the feelings you have at home enhance your work experience? You do realize that from the moment your son drew his first breath love impacted his life. Look at the effect it had."

Sage nodded in agreement.

MJ continued. "Just feeding, swaddling, and sheltering an infant isn't enough to ensure his or her survival. Failure to thrive in a newborn can often be traced to a lack of loving contact and the emotional commitment of another person. From my perspective, Sage, most business failures, marriage failures, and poor relationships can also be traced to a lack of loving touch or emotional commitment."

Sage was nodding in agreement, but not with total commitment. "Really?"

"From where I sit," MJ went on, "it's six one way, half dozen the other. So yes, really. Ask yourself, what's love got to do with it?"

"It seems pretty clear when you put it like that," Sage said.

"I don't want you to get the impression that because a person loves what they do and are intensely committed to it that the consequences of their involvement will always be positive. Fidel Castro was committed to the revolution and loved his country, but there are a lot of people who would take issue with the goodness of his efforts. History is replete with examples of people who thought what they were doing was good and right—for love of country, love of faith, religion, or their races—yet their efforts were foolhardy at best and ultimately proved to be folly."

"Let me ask you this. What is the most prevalent complaint of American workers?" MJ queried.

"Well," Sage began, "I know what they complain about where I work. 'They don't get enough time off, and the food is for crap.'" They both laughed.

"I suppose those are two pretty good things to carp about," MJ agreed. "But across the board, employees complain about *not being in the loop*. They have no idea what's going on because management doesn't talk to them."

"They feel left out," Sage added.

"Exactly," MJ said. "Everyone wants to believe they're important. They want to be informed, and they want to be involved. But more than that, they want to be valued. They want to know that somebody cares."

"That makes sense," Sage said.

"We make time for the things that are important to us," MJ continued. "Everybody knows that. So when the boss doesn't take the time to talk with an employee—to try to understand what concerns him or her—it effectively says the administration's got no love for them."

"Sure," Sage put in. "Your actions have to back your words. You can say you value other people's opinions all you want, but if you never take time to listen, it's just empty rhetoric, mere words."

"Right again," MJ said. "The very same thing happens in negotiations. Facilitators need to be committed to the people they're working with. If a facilitator doesn't care about what they're doing or with whom they're doing it, it'll show. Their actions will make it obvious that they care more about the metrics than the people."

"Come on now, it's important to focus on metrics," Sage protested. "Our success is dependent on how well we meet or exceed the standards and the organization's metric values. It's how we know whether we're winning or not."

MJ scrunched up her face so that her forehead creased, drawing her eyebrows together. "You're not one of those people whose success is tied to a dollar metric, are you?" Without waiting for an answer, she continued, "Because if you are, you might want to remind yourself that money isn't everything."

"Oh, no, uh-uh," Sage said, thrusting her hands out in front of her defensively. "That's not me. Although, I had an aunt who liked to say, 'What money can't buy, I don't want.'" Both women grinned. "Actually, I don't care all that much about money. I mean, I know I need it to exist, but it's just not all that important to what I really care about. Sometimes it seems like I give more away than I keep."

"Well, okay then," MJ said, looking somewhat relieved. "Having said that, I hope you don't think I'm telling you to throw everything to the wind, find a tree to embrace, or meditate until you sweat, trying to discover the meaning of life."

Sage chuckled. "No, I didn't get that impression."

"Whew. That wouldn't have been an artful display of communication on my part. You see, I believe in wealth and I adore prosperity. Financial reward is a good thing, but it's not *every*thing. What I'm saying is, if you live well, listen, communicate, and love well, there's no reason you can't have it all, money included. Or a good share of it anyway.

"What I'm talking about is taking advantage of your abilities. As a negotiator, facilitator, mother, sister, father, brother you simply must be at your level best when interacting with others. That requires commitment. Good facilitators interact purposefully to expand their knowledge, asking pertinent questions and providing appropriate feedback so they better understand the wants, needs and desires of those with whom they interact. This is to everyone's advantage. That will make you someone others will look up to and willingly follow."

MJ took a breath before continuing. "The passion you demonstrate for what you do can be infectious. Your enthusiasm and commitment can inspire others to work harder so they finish well."

"Ah, so we're back to love, huh?" Sage asked, half-jokingly.

MJ got up from her chair and went to look out her office window. "I get it," she said, then turned around to face Sage again. "You're thinking, 'I can't believe this woman is asking me to send flowers and blow kisses as a mediation strategy.'"

Sage smiled, because she'd been nailed in her doubt.

MJ smiled as well. "Kisses are good," she said, "but I'd suggest you save those for your husband. I'm not suggesting you open discussions by telling everyone how much you *looooove* them or other such mawkish drivel. That'll only make you look silly and give people something to talk about once you leave."

Sage started grinning again, and it soon turned into a full-bodied laugh. MJ started laughing too. It was infectious. Trying to regain her composure while wiping tears from the corners of her eyes, MJ attempted to speak. It didn't work very well at first, but she kept at it until it did. She took a deep breath, then started again.

"Sure," she said, as she wiped at her eyes again, "timely and well-placed praise can work wonders for an ego and jumpstart the momentum in an otherwise stalled interaction. What you say and do—verbally and nonverbally—will keep things moving or not."

"I agree," Sage said. "Our words and deeds have to be consistent. And nix any declarations or public displays of affection." She started to chuckle again but managed to keep her composure.

"Right," said MJ. "One of the things I find most interesting about negotiations is that there are times you'll lead, and others when you'll need to hang back and let someone else do the leading. What I'm saying is that sometimes the best way to lead is to *follow.*"

MJ turned and thoughtfully looked out of the window again. "My brother taught me that," she said. "We were working with some friends, and apparently I was being a little too pushy because he pulled me aside. He steered me toward this guy I'd never met. On the way, he said under his breath, 'In order to lead, you first must learn to follow.' Then he introduced us. While I wouldn't have guessed it at the time, the man ended up being my husband. I think my brother planned it that way, the brat."

Sage started chuckling. She tried to hold it in but soon the two of them started laughing again.

Still smiling, MJ said, "I think I've got the 'following' thing down now. Or then again, maybe not. But I let my husband think I do. It makes him happy, so…" she trailed off, and let it go. Continuing a moment later, she said, "I remind myself every now and again that even when I think I'm *following*, someone is likely watching and *taking my lead.*"

She sat down and leaned back. "Inevitably, you'll develop a relationship, of some sort, with the people you meet. And any relationship you forge, good or bad, will impact your ability to succeed. The nature of your relationships can either facilitate or impede your ability to get where you want to go. So, what I am advising is to be open to compassion and nurture your relationships. Accept the challenge to lead, know when to follow, and when to allow personal growth by being still." She looked off as if remembering something important. "Got it?" she asked.

Sage knew that "Got it" was rhetorical, so she didn't bother answering. Instead, she waited for MJ to continue, which she promptly did.

"You should be vigilant to ensure your expectations are clearly understood. And really take the time to understand other people's positions and the rationale they use to support them. If you don't, more often than not you'll be dissatisfied with what comes back at you. This is where the empathy thing we talked about comes in. You'll need to get in the other person's skin and move around a bit until it fits."

"Sometimes it's hard to know what people are trying to tell you," Sage said. "Try as I might, there are occasions when the crux of what one side or the other is attempting to get across escapes me."

"Maybe it's because they don't know what they're trying to say either," MJ said, nodding as if she knew exactly what Sage was talking about.

"It pains me to admit it," Sage confessed, "but there are times the rhetoric gets so intense I just want to get the heck out."

"Been there, done that," MJ responded. "It happens to all of us. You just need to remind yourself that much of what you'll get will be hyperbole. One side will present an exaggerated position, with no explanation, and get insulted when the other side presents a counter argument that's equally unreasonable. In cases like that, you and I can spend a lot of time talking to no effect. Just remember this: Sometimes the people who talk the most say the least. Lots of talking doesn't necessarily make for a good interaction. That requires purposeful, meaningful discussion with lots of listening, verification, analyzing, and acknowledgment."

"That makes sense," Sage murmured.

"So, there you have it. The way you listen and communicate is key to building healthy, wholesome relationships."

Sage looked off for a moment, recalling both good and bad examples of mediations she'd facilitated. Then she turned to MJ and said, "This is a lot to take in."

"Should I stop, or would you like me to go on."

"Don't stop," Sage said. "I was just thinking out loud."

MJ settled herself as she contemplated where to pick up. She had gone over quite a bit. *I should probably not take this too much further today*, she thought to herself.

4

Active Intelligent Listening

"Do you realize how much time people spend spouting rhetoric?" MJ asked.

"Well, yeah. I think I do."

"You do realize then that nothing I've said up to now has been primarily focused on rhetoric?" MJ asked.

"Okay," replied Sage.

MJ then emphasized how important it was for Sage to realize that every interaction entailed more than the rhetoric espoused during the discussion. She said, "When people don't really listen, any conversation can become a war of words or worse. When people become contentious and neither side is willing to relent, nasty things can happen. And that, my dear, is why you and I have jobs."

"Every war ends in one of three ways: annihilation, occupation, or communication. I use the term 'war' to refer to *any* adversarial interaction, including the real thing. What's important for you to remember is that confrontation can only be resolved in one of these ways."

MJ took a sip of her drink, brushed her hair to the side, and said, "The worst possible outcome of disagreement, 'war,' that is, is being annihilated." She rubbed her hand through her hair once more, then down the side of her face. "Annihilation is nothing less than the purposeful destruction of another's position. Some people can make sound arguments for just about any position they take. Others may have difficulty making arguments that can withstand even the most meager opposition. Whether it's done with vocabulary, erudition, or sheer force of presence, if you decimate a person's position, you'll alienate them and minimize any opportunity to affect an empathetic understanding, develop a sense of unity, or otherwise gain their commitment."

"If I've seen it once, I've seen it a hundred times," Sage agreed.

"Me, too," MJ lamented, "and it's never pretty. Unfortunately, being occupied can feel almost as bad, if not worse, in the long run."

"How can you occupy another person?" Sage asked.

"Occupation occurs when both sides are relatively secure in their positions and similarly proficient. Neither side is able to get the other to alter their position or to lessen their resolve. In effect," MJ continued, "when neither side is capable of defeating the other, they start looking for a way out.

This typically results in one side offering something of value to the other in exchange for something they value themselves. Such exchanges are rarely equitable or satisfying."

"You're talking about a compromise, aren't you?" Sage asked.

"That's pretty much it. Yes."

"When people can't move, but they're in each other's space, they do what they can to make things less uncomfortable. If they give something to the other side and get a little something in return, they can allow themselves to feel as if they've won. That is at least a small victory."

"Most of my mediations have ended like that," Sage said. "And you know what's amazing to me is that I've not once looked at it this way before. I guess that explains why people always leave my settlements unhappy."

MJ merely smiled.

"It makes so much sense when you think about it," Sage said. "What's the solution?"

"The solution," MJ said, "the last best chance we have to ensure everyone gets what they need is simply by talking with each other and honestly listening."

"Open honest discussion. I get it," Sage said.

"I have no doubt you do," MJ affirmed. "Effective interactions are an absolute must. Every participant has to decide how he or she wants an interaction to end. To end well they need to trust each other. Trust is prerequisite to attaining an empathetic understanding. You need to listen intently enough to fully understand what you're being told. It's what I call *Active Intelligent Listening.* That's what it takes to open a door that'll allow everyone to win."

"Hold on!" Sage interjected. "What's 'Active Intelligent Listening'?"

"It's the act of intently focusing on what a person is saying to acquire an empathetic understanding of their reasoning without prejudice of position," MJ told her.

"Whoa!" Sage said, interrupting MJ's train of thought for the second time. "That went by awfully fast. I need you to do that again."

"No problem," MJ said. "Active Intelligent Listening involves more than just listening to what's being said. You must look for nonverbal expressions that provide color, clarity, and conscience to the conversation. The idea is to listen discriminatingly, for inflection, for tone, and with your eyes for body language and physical signs of stress, emotion or resolve. In other words, you need to listen with all your senses, giving the person speaking your full attention.

"The concept's been around like... forever." MJ motioned over her shoulder to a quote she had hanging on the wall. It read: *Could a greater miracle take place than for us to look through each other's eye for an instant?*

"You see that?" MJ continued. "That's Thoreau. Henry David Thoreau. He was talking about seeing what others see, through their eyes. Listening with their ears.

He's telling you to feel what they feel, with their heart. That's what 'Active Intelligent Listening' is. It requires the use of more than your ears. It involves the use of your eyes, and intuition. You need to interpret a person's body language, be aware of their condition. For example, are they sweating? Are they tearing up? And you can analyze their vocal inflections."

"It's an acquired skill, no doubt," Sage opined. "One of those that takes lots of practice and patience, I bet." She smiled. MJ returned it warmly.

"Haven't you found it to be true," MJ asked, "not just in mediation, but with any disagreement, that people generally begin developing their rebuttal instead of paying attention to what the other person is telling them?"

"Yeah," said Sage. "I've been guilty of it myself on more than one occasion."

"You're not alone," MJ replied. "All too often, when one person says something another disagrees with, they stop listening and start constructing a counter-argument. If you're observant you'll catch the nonverbals well before he or she even opens his or her mouth."

"I read somewhere that approximately 93 percent of communication is nonverbal," Sage interjected.

"If you're not paying attention, you could miss some very important unspoken messages," MJ added. "Although that '93 percent' number is a questionable statistic at best. The point is, simple things like voice inflection speak volumes about a person's intentions."

"You mean like when someone tells you to 'Have a nice day'?" Sage offered. "On the one hand, they could mean exactly that. But they could also be telling you to take a flying leap.

"Absolutely," MJ said. "The only way to know the difference is to *listen* to their voice inflection and *watch* the body language. Like crossing your arms and legs might tell me that you don't care what I'm saying. The look on your face might reinforce that message. But if I'm not paying attention, I could just as easily assume you were listening intently to everything I said."

"I took a class on 'body language' once," Sage said. "I remember thinking I'd never use it. But you're right. I've probably missed some very important nonverbal clues even though I thought I was giving the speaker my full attention."

"You and me both," MJ said. "We like to fool ourselves into believing that we're really good listeners. But if you're not watching everything a person does or paying close attention to the subtle changes in their tone and/or inflections, you can miss a lot."

"So, that was a long answer to a short question. Just remember," MJ continued, "'Active Intelligent Listening' means you're focused intently on what the speaker is saying and at the same time watching, with equal intensity, what they're doing. Block out extraneous or distracting thoughts. That's how you get to an empathetic understanding. And that's it."

"Practice and patience," Sage replied without hesitation. "You see? I *have* been listening."

"So you have," MJ said, "so you have." She glanced at the clock on the wall. "I'm afraid time has gotten away from us." She paused for a moment, then went to her desk and checked her calendar. Looking up, she asked, "Would you like to sit in on a mediation I'm doing next week?"

"I'd love to," Sage responded, surprised at how honestly eager she was for the opportunity. "Your last session must have been something—though I have yet to figure out exactly what happened."

"It took me a while to put this strategy together," MJ said. "It might take you a moment or two to figure it out. I have to finalize a couple of things yet, but I'll call tomorrow and give you the time, date, and the place."

"I'd like that," Sage replied, standing and moving towards the door.

"Tomorrow then." MJ said, extending her hand.

Sage reached out and gently accepted MJ's hand. They didn't really shake hands. They merely held on to each other for a moment. "Tomorrow, then," Sage said as she released her grip and started towards the door. Her head was swimming with ideas. But she liked to swim, so it was okay.

❖

Every War Ends in One of Three Ways

Annihilation

The absolute destruction of another's
position, purpose, or person

Occupation

The coexistence in relative spaces and time with
exchanges for convenience or acquiescence

Communication

The act of listening to and exchanging ideas, concepts
and proposals for the mutual benefit, satisfaction, and
enhancement of everyone involved

❖

5

The Problem with Compromise

Franklin Pennimore appeared to be softening, albeit not much. MJ was just closing the session for the day. Frank grumbled to himself. The other participants agreed to continue the mediation the following week. They set the time and date and got Frank to acquiesce, if reluctantly. Frank made it clear he wasn't happy about the way things were going. Glowering at the people in the room, he muttered, "We've got some serious work to do here." He was still grumbling as he passed Sage and ambled out of the room. Sage swiveled her chair to face MJ. Casually rocking back and forth, Sage was ruminating on the events of the day, caught up in her thoughts.

"Why so pensive?" MJ asked.

Somewhat startled, Sage looked up. "Huh?" she grunted.

"I'm sorry. I was trying to make sense of the way this turned out. It went pretty much the same as most mediations I either sat through or conducted myself—badly! After your last session went so well, I was expecting something more, something different...." She paused for a moment. "I don't know...something better. That's all."

"It wasn't that bad," MJ said.

"Come again?"

"Well look," MJ said, "we've scheduled another meeting, and we made a little progress. So let's just wait and see how things go next week."

"Next week?" Sage asked sarcastically. "Do you really think Frank will be any less difficult to deal with a week from now?"

"Well, I don't think he held anything back today, that's for sure," MJ said, smiling. "But that's not necessarily a bad thing. Frank got an opportunity to tell his story. Everybody has one, and today Frank got to share his. Sometimes people can get pretty worked up when they're letting it all out." MJ shoved a few papers into her briefcase.

"So now," she said, looking at Sage, and holding up three fingers, "I have three questions that I need Frank to answer." She began checking them off on her fingers. "First, he needs to be specific in telling us *why* he feels the way he does. Second, he needs to articulate *exactly* what he wants. And third, he needs to tell us *why* he believes getting what he wants will satisfy his needs and *if* he can see any other ways to get there." She took her free hand, folded her extended fingers into a fist, and covered them with her other hand. "Actually, that's four questions," she said, grinning. "I hate it when it does that."

Chuckling, Sage said, "After listening to Frank, I'm not sure anything will make him happy. He seems perfectly content standing his ground."

"There's nothing new here," MJ said. "You've experienced this sort of interaction before, haven't you?" The question was rhetorical.

"You know I have," Sage nodded. "And when I'm dealing with someone as recalcitrant as Frank, we usually end up either deadlocked or one side gets beaten up pretty badly."

"Yeah, and there's a reason people like Frank act the way they do," MJ said. "Some folks are pretty disillusioned with compromising. It's a lot more appealing these days to embrace outright confrontation than to be conciliatory. That's partly, I think, because the consequences of compromise have been so notoriously mediocre. That makes standing one's ground an appealing alternative."

"That's probably true," Sage consented.

"No, not probably," MJ said. "Absolutely. I can point to hundreds of examples. They're everywhere." She opened her arms to indicate the area around them. "There have been times when a presidential nominee vacated his or her position and everyone in the senate lost their mind," she continued. "This phenomenon is completely unmasked at times like that."

"Yes, I remember," Sage said. "I think I know what you're getting at. I remember a time when the Senate Majority absolutely refused to entertain the notion of giving a confirmation hearing to anyone the current president nominated to fill an open position."

"Precisely," MJ added. "Instead of a fair and impartial hearing, the Senate chose to stymie the appointment by not even talking about it. The system worked against itself because compromise was viewed as an ineffective strategy."

"Seems so," Sage said. "Our elected officials have, what? Compromised themselves into a perpetual state of mortal conflict?"

"That's one way to put it," MJ replied. While still tidying up, she continued, "Rather than compromise, some people will either refuse to engage or refuse to entertain an alternative. In so doing, they either force a stalemate or force a fight that continues until one side or the other cries 'uncle.'"

"So, it's either deadlock or defeat." Sage said sadly. It was more a statement than a question.

"That's very true," MJ agreed. "And that could just as easily happen here...with Frank. But I'm an optimist." She smiled. "Anyway, we got some things out in the open today. So let's be patient and see how it goes next week. Why don't we continue this conversation over dinner?" MJ glanced at Sage. "Want to grab something to eat?"

"Sure," Sage answered. "I could use a little something."

"Good. I'm meeting a friend for dinner. I think he may be able to give you some insights into compromise you may not have thought about. He does this for a living, too. Mediation, I mean."

Sage hesitated for a moment. "Are you sure it's okay?" she asked. "I don't want to be a third wheel."

"Not that kind of relationship," MJ said. "We're just good friends. It'll be fine. He likes to meet new people. Says it broadens his horizons." She offered a smile that went all the way to her eyes. "Michael has good instincts. I think you'll like him."

* * * * *

The food was good enough, but the restaurant was a little loud. Sage had to strain to hear Michael as he spoke. "I'm sorry," she said. "Could you say that again?"

"No problem," he told her. Michael started over, a little louder this time. "Look," he said, "we've been told all our lives that compromise is a good thing. Everybody wins, right? Yet if you look closely, you'll see that with every compromise you usually end up giving more than you'd have liked. People are tired of compromising and giving in. It's just losing by another name. So rather than lose all the time, they become hostile. The idea being that if they play tough, maybe they'll win for a change. Look, intuitively we know compromise is a losing proposition. That's why nobody is particularly happy with it. But if you fight, you stand a chance of winning. You could lose as well, but with compromise you're definitely gonna lose something. And frankly, people are tired of losing. At least I know I am."

"You've only to look at what's happening in D.C.," MJ offered. "Gridlock. Nothing gets done. They just keep snipping at one another."

"Case-in-point," Michael said. "No one's willing to compromise because they know it means they'll have to give something away that won't leave them happy.

"But sacrificing for the greater good is a sign of selflessness, isn't it?" Sage asked. "It's a good thing."

"If you give something for what you believe to be a greater good, is it a sacrifice?" Michael said as he and MJ looked at each other and smiled as if sharing a special secret.

"Okay, what? Did I say something amusing?" Sage asked, shifting her attention from one dinner companion to the other.

MJ looked at Michael and said, "No, not really. It's just…well, I'll let Michael explain it."

"That's just like you," Michael said, "start something and then expect me to finish it."

"Oh, come on, Mikey, you do this so well."

"That's enough with the 'Mikey' stuff," he said. He looked at Sage and told her, "Ignore that person over there. She ain't right. You can dress her up but don't even think about trying to take her anywhere."

Sage volleyed her gaze from one to the other hoping they weren't going to leave her hanging.

Michael held up his right index finger and pointed at MJ across the table. "What that one wants me to do is ask you a couple of questions."

"Okay," Sage said. "Ask me what?"

"She wants me to ask you which of your principles you're willing to compromise?"

"Which of my *principles*?" Sage asked incredulously.

"Yes," Michael said. "Tell us which of your principles you are willing to violate to satisfy someone else's interests."

Sage gave it a moment's thought. "I won't compromise my principles," Sage answered.

"And why is that?" Michael asked.

"Because," Sage said.

"Because…why?" Michael asked with a hint of a smile pulling at one corner of his mouth.

"Because principles are sacred," Sage told him. "My father once told me that 'To compromise a single principle is to deny the existence of any.' I don't know where he borrowed that quote from. He didn't say. But what he did say was that my principles define who I am, and I should never give up who I am to satisfy someone else. I've taken that to heart. I won't compromise my principles."

"How about your religious beliefs? Will you compromise those?" Michael asked.

"No."

"Your children? Are you willing to compromise the safety of your children for a righteous cause?"

"No," Sage snapped, somewhat indignantly.

MJ didn't wait for Michael to continue before bursting in, "What are you willing to compromise—that's important to you, I mean?" she asked.

"Well, I can't think of anything right now," Sage said.

"Take your time," Michael said. "I need to order some dessert anyway. I gotta have something sweet after a good meal. You want anything?" he asked his two dinner partners, looking from one to the other.

"I'm having tiramisu," MJ said as she glanced Sage's way.

Sage didn't respond. She was too busy trying to think of something she cared about but was willing to compromise for someone else's benefit.

"If you were put in the right situation, you would most likely compromise something you cared about," Michael said. "After all, that's been drilled into your head your entire life. And you've been doing it for years. *Compromise is the way we get things done. It's become the foundation of our politics.* But that hasn't been working for us in Washington, has it?"

Sage shrugged, still trying to think of something she'd willfully give up for the sake of compromise.

Michael didn't wait for her answer. "Compromise is a measure of mediocrity," he declared. "Greatness has never been a byproduct of compromise. In fact, greatness cannot be achieved through compromise."

"That's a pretty strong assertion, Michael," said Sage.

"It is," he said. "So okay, name any great chef who is willing to compromise one of his or her special recipes. I'm not talking about experimentation. I'm talking about substitution, adding, or subtracting. For instance, what kind of chef would substitute cod, which is considered the poor man's lobster, for the real thing?"

Sage tried to think of an example as Michael waved a dismissive hand and kept on going. "JFK didn't compromise when he set his sights on going to the moon. Roger Bannister didn't compromise his training or his goal of running a sub-four-minute mile. NASA didn't compromise on the safety requirements for the space shuttle. Gandhi didn't compromise. Dr. King didn't compromise. And neither did Nelson Mandela."

Sage wasn't sure about this. *They must have had to compromise something, didn't they?* She tried to think of an example but wasn't having much luck. It didn't matter because Michael didn't give her any quarter.

"How about this?" he continued. "Can you find a single chapter or verse anywhere in the Bible suggesting Jesus compromised?"

"Ask the money-changers." MJ chimed in chuckling.

"You can't compromise the *truth*. You can't compromise *loyalty*. You can't compromise *friendship, love, fidelity, or infinity*." He paused, enjoying his somewhat theatrical flourish.

MJ broke the silence. "I agree with Michael," she said.

"The only things you should compromise are those that don't matter. If you compromise your character, you sacrifice something about yourself that leaves you the lesser for it. If you compromise your esteem, your commitment, your dedication, some part of you is lessened," she told them.

"Greatness can only be achieved through the transcendence of tension, conflict, and adversity," Michael added. "Never through compromise."

"Wait a minute," Sage said, forming a "T" with her hands for "time-out." "How about we define compromise so we're on the same page?

"Good enough," Michael replied. "Voltaire once said, 'If you would argue with me, define your terms.' Okay. So what do you think 'compromise' means?"

Sage thought. "Umm...finding common ground?" she suggested.

Both Michael and MJ shook their heads.

"That's what you would *like* it to mean," MJ said. "Let's get the dictionary definition." Pulling out her cell phone, she murmured, "The *modern* dictionary." Using her thumbs, she typed "definition for compromise." She read what came up.

"Okay, compromise—the first definition says: 'To settle a dispute by mutual concession.' What does the dictionary say about conceding? Here it is," she said, "concede: 'To surrender or yield something that one possesses.' Let's go back to compromise. Second definition: 'To accept standards that are lower than is desirable.' That doesn't sound good." Continuing, MJ read on. "It says here that compromise comes from a French word meaning to consent to an arbitration! I guess that means compromise is at the heart of every arbitration," MJ concluded.

"So then," Sage put in. "Arbitration involves compromise?"

"Yeah, but nobody wins." Michael said. "Nobody wins with compromise. It's self-defeating to relinquish something you relish in hopes of getting something else you can just live with. The very act of sacrificing something of value will leave a bitter taste in your mouth. That's why no one seems happy after completing a mediation where compromise ruled the day."

"But what about finding *common ground*—a place where both sides agree?" Sage offered.

"There's a difference between 'compromise' and 'agreement'," Michael said. "The key is the word 'common.' If something is common, it's shared. Both sides have it. There's no need to compromise because the parties already share what they're purportedly seeking."

"'Common ground,' metaphorically speaking, is a place both parties can plant their feet. Not one standing on top of the other, but side by side with substantially similar interests."

Sage was muttering to herself, but it came out loud enough for her dinner companions to pick it up. "I see.

'Common'... we both have it. We understand it the same."
Nodding thoughtfully, she said aloud, "There is no
difference. 'Common ground' is shared ground. We're on
it together."

"Absolutely!" Michael exclaimed, jumping in again,
"We should be flexible. But there's a difference between
changing your mind because you have better information
and deciding inflexibly for the sake of appeasement.
You know what I mean. Go along to get along. Winston
Churchill once said, an 'appeaser' is 'one who feeds a
crocodile, hoping it will eat him last.'" They all laughed.

While still laughing, Sage said, "I guess he would
have known."

"Yeah, I think he would have," Michael said.
"Altering one's thinking isn't the same as compromising.
Compromise is avoidance behavior. Anyone can avoid
making the tough decisions. It takes courage and
commitment to work through the difficult machinations
that lead to understanding and to make decisions based
on what's good and right. Good and right for both
parties."

Across the table MJ was nodding in agreement and
watching for Sage's reaction. Michael went on. "Now, it's
possible to come up with the same solution when you
work to understand something as you may have through
compromise. The difference is that when you compromise,
you sacrifice or surrender something. When you reach a

level of understanding and do that which you know to be good and right, you sacrifice nothing. You willingly and willfully give for the greater good."

The waiter interrupted the conversation to bring their desserts. Sage hadn't ordered anything. She'd been too deep in thought to place an order. She looked at MJ's tiramisu and then at Michael's Key lime pie. "That pie looks good," she said.

"Want some?" he asked. "I'll get the waiter for you."

"No," she responded. "I couldn't eat a whole piece of pie right now."

"No problem," Michael said. "You can have some of mine." He smiled at her.

"Didn't you just get through telling me that compromise doesn't work?" Sage asked.

"Sure," Michael said. "But letting you have a piece of my pie isn't a compromise. It's not a compromise if you do something because you *want* to. Sharing is being a good friend, not compromising. Changing your position because you recognize a greater good also changes your perception for the potential outcome. Which means you make a commitment, not a sacrifice.

"It's called free will. Freedom can't be coerced: there's no quid pro quo. You don't have to give something to get something."

Gesturing to the plate in front of him, Michael said, "I don't really need all of this pie. If I eat it, I'll need to run another mile-and-a-half in the morning, which I really don't want to do. And you can't eat a whole piece of pie. So, it doesn't make sense for you to order one. Recognizing this, I understand it to be in our best interest for me to share my pie with you. We both win. I won't need to run another mile-and-a-half, and you won't pay to waste half a piece of pie. We all leave happy."

"That is, if I actually get a piece of that pie," Sage quipped.

Laughing, Michael pushed his plate towards the center of the table. Picking up her fork, Sage dug in. "I appreciate the fact that you didn't have to compromise," she said, raising the pie-laden fork to her lips.

6

Getting What They Want

The tension in the room was palpable. Frank's demeanor suggested he'd been stewing since the last session and was ready for battle. He started to speak, but MJ interjected before he could get two words out. "I'm sorry to interrupt you, Frank, but I need to make sure I'm on the right track before we get started."

"Well…okay," Frank said, leaning reluctantly back in his chair.

"I just want to take a couple of minutes to make sure I understood your position correctly," she began. "Last week you told us…" MJ then recited Frank's story back to him much as he'd presented it during the previous meeting. "Did I get that right?" she asked. "Was I able to understand your position as you intended?"

"Well, yes," Frank replied, a little surprised. "Yes, you did."

MJ looked around the room and asked if anyone had gotten a different impression. Everyone indicated they were pretty much of the same mind. There were a couple of questions, which led Frank to clarify some of his stated positions. He even apologized for what he characterized as an un-artful representation. The discussion was entirely non-confrontational. Sage was intrigued while she watched the exchange. It was difficult to believe this was the same man who'd been loaded for bear a few minutes ago.

MJ turned to the group and suggested they focus on ways to help Frank get what he needed without sacrificing their own needs. She then gave Frank an opportunity to respond to the four questions she'd mentioned to Sage the previous week. MJ asked him to explain specifically *why* he felt the way he did and what he wanted. She then gave Frank an opportunity to explain *why* he believed that if he got what he asked for, that his needs would be satisfied.

MJ explained to the group the importance of knowing what success looked like from their perspective, and what it meant in real terms. She emphasized the importance of not getting married to one solution but rather to look for similarly effective alternatives.

Once Frank finished, the group began looking for solutions that wouldn't compromise his position. Several modified their own thinking as they took in new and/or better information.

The process was repeated for any who felt they needed further consideration.

It was a long day. The results however, were surprisingly good. Sage noted the looks of satisfaction on the people's faces as the day wrapped up.

"Okay," Sage said as the participants filed out. "That went a lot more like the first mediation. How did you get Frank to engage like that?"

"I let him know he'd been heard," MJ explained. "Do you recall how the session began?"

"You recounted the story Frank told us last week," Sage said.

"And?"

"And what?"

"And I reinforced the fact that he'd been *heard*," MJ said. "Everyone in the room confirmed that my recitation was factually representative of what Frank told us last week. Frank felt like he was being validated. He saw that everybody in the room had listened to his story. They had considered the implications for a week and confirmed what they understood him to have said. Then they all agreed to help Frank find a solution that didn't require him to compromise."

"Yeah," Sage interrupted. "Then Frank started trying to make sure that no one else had to compromise either. Wow."

"Everybody looking out for everybody else," MJ agreed. "What's important here is that when everyone involved is trying to help you and you're trying to help everyone else, everybody wins. No one is left out."

"I'd almost given up trying to find a way that everyone could actually win," Sage said, incredulous.

"When a person tries to make things better for him or herself," MJ continued, "he or she often makes things worse for someone else. Typically, feathers get ruffled. But when a person takes the time to make someone *else's* position better, the affected party is likely to reciprocate. Then magic happens." She smiled. "If there are ten people involved, nine others are working to make things better for the tenth. That's what happens when people are selfless as opposed to selfish. Everybody hates the person who makes their job harder. But they'll like anyone who makes their work easier."

Sage looked at MJ and said, "*It's not about you! Never has been and never will be.* I wasn't exactly sure what you were getting at when you first told me that. I get it now. What a concept. By helping others, people will appreciate what I do more than they would if I was merely helping myself."

"It's easy to like people who are good to you," MJ said. "Not so much those who only look out for themselves." MJ paused for a moment. "So, back to Frank. He came in a little on the pugnacious side. You did notice that, right?"

"I sure did," Sage said. "And so did everyone else in the room. I think some of the others were locked and loaded as well."

"But Frank's resistance eased once he realized that people had listened to his story and were willing to help. Now some of the others probably *hadn't* listened," MJ said, waving a hand dismissively. "Almost certainly not as carefully as *I* had. But I recounted his story accurately. That way, when I asked the others if they remembered it as I had, everyone who said yes reinforced the notion that they had also listened. By doing so, I helped Frank see the other people in the room as advocates and not as adversaries. Did you notice that?"

Sage nodded.

MJ continued, "I got everyone to help Frank resolve his problem without him having to compromise."

"So Frank saw he was not alone," Sage offered. "Everybody in the room was committed to helping him get what he needed."

"Without sacrifice," MJ added. "And they got to do it without compromising their needs either. When Frank came in, he believed the only way to get what he needed was either to compromise, meaning sacrificing something he really wanted to keep—which he really didn't want to do—or to dig in. Confrontation was preferable to compromise because he'd at least have a chance to win."

"And compromise didn't give him that chance," Sage said.

"No, it did not," MJ agreed. "I had to *reframe* the discussion," she explained. "I had to give Frank a reason to believe he could win without fighting. I needed to get Frank to think on a different level."

"What do you mean by different level?" Sage asked.

"There are basically three levels on which people interact," MJ said. The first level is confrontational and is driven entirely by emotion. It's the equivalent of 'annihilating' the opposition. Level Two is conciliatory and seeks compromise. This is acquiescing, which is akin to 'occupation'. It's driven by emotion and tempered by rationality. Level Three looks toward developing an empathetic understanding. This is where the magic happens. It's all about effective communication."

"You've mentioned empathetic understanding before," Sage said.

"I have," MJ answered. "Empathy enhances our understanding, allowing us to make decisions that don't compromise the interest of other people. Communicating at Level Three requires greater interaction and commitment than the other two levels. It's a great deal more cerebral and significantly less emotional."

MJ paused for a moment to take a deep breath. "Now that doesn't mean Level Three is without passion. People can be very passionate about their beliefs. Just because they're interacting at Level Three doesn't mean they'll do it without passion. Level Three interactions just don't allow anything to derail the rationality of the discourse.

Frank walked in here today looking to engage at Level One, but he ended up on Level Three."

Sage smiled, recalling what she'd seen. "Today was great and completely unexpected," she said. "I need you to tell me more about these levels though. I'm curious as to how they influence the way people talk to each other. And I really want to know how to get from one level to another and how you know when it's time to make that move. Will you help me with that?"

"Of course I will," MJ said. "But it's going to take some time. Perhaps another day."

"Okay," Sage replied, a bit disheartened. "Let me know what's good for you. I'll be ready."

MJ agreed. They said their goodbyes and left for the evening. Sage was still playing the events of the day over in her head.

Three Levels of Interaction

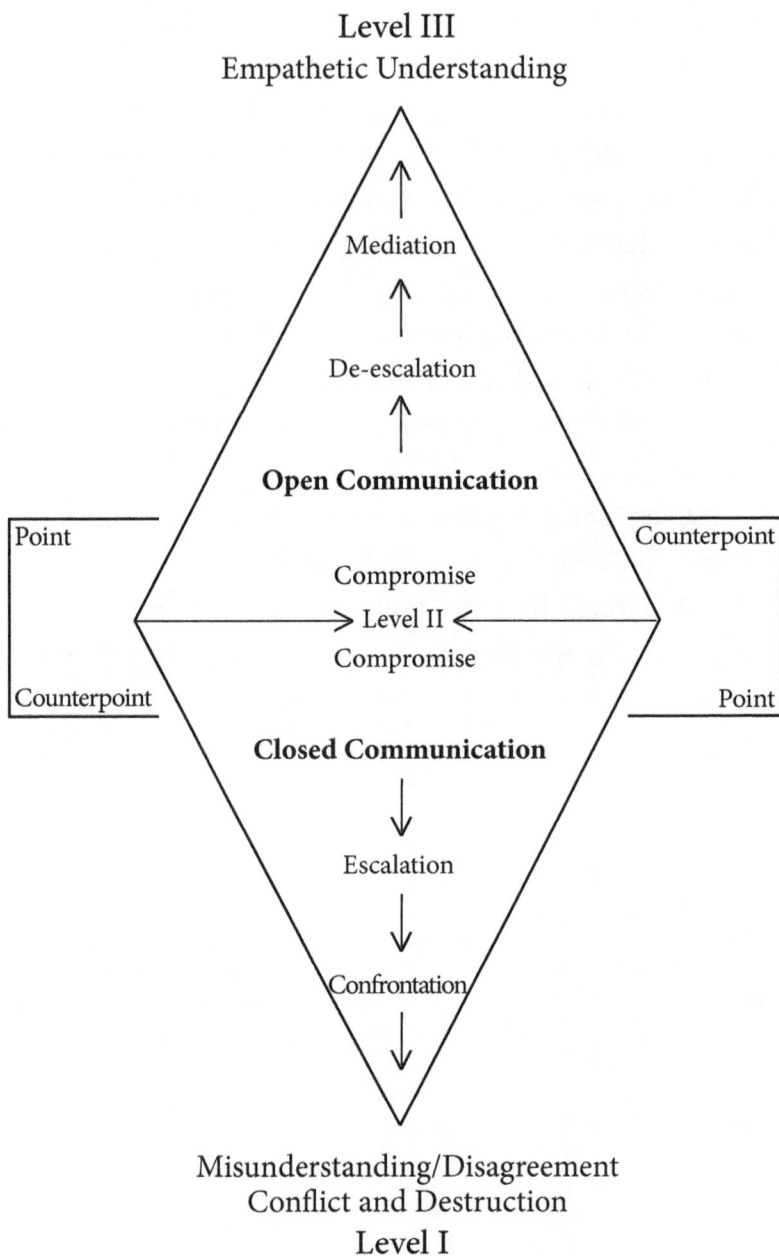

Level III
Empathetic Understanding

Mediation

↑

De-escalation

↑

Open Communication

Point   Counterpoint

Compromise
Level II ←
Compromise

Counterpoint   Point

Closed Communication

↓

Escalation

↓

Confrontation

↓

Misunderstanding/Disagreement
Conflict and Destruction
Level I

7

Confrontation: Level I Interactions

Sage sauntered through the racks of clothing and assorted knickknacks, enjoying the hustle-bustle of *Sidewalk Days*. She'd been tempted to buy something she didn't need but managed to resist the urge. The aroma coming from the open-air cafés made her mouth water. She was thinking of getting a latté when someone called out to her. Sage scanned the area to see who it was but didn't see anyone she knew. She heard her name again. Looking over her shoulder, she saw Michael waving a hand to get her attention. He was sitting under a colorfully striped umbrella, sipping a drink.

"Good morning," Michael said, motioning for Sage to join him. "I was just thinking about our conversation from the other night, and here you are."

"And I was just thinking about getting a latté," smiled Sage, gesturing to Michael's cup.

"Great minds," Michael offered, raising his cup. "Care to join me?"

"Thanks," Sage said, nodding and pulling one of the hand-woven chairs from under the table.

"Not having any luck?" Michael asked. Sage looked at him, uncertain of what he meant.

"Shopping," he clarified. "You're not carrying any bags. I thought perhaps you weren't having any luck finding what you were looking for."

"Oh, I was just browsing," Sage said. "Sidewalk Days are a good time to get away. I like looking for sales and watching people."

"I like them, too. But more for the food and drink than the shopping."

A waitress interrupted. "Can I get you anything?" she asked Sage.

"I'll have a small iced, non-fat, vanilla latté," Sage answered. "And a piece of banana walnut bread please."

"Of course," the waitress said, as she placed a napkin on the table in front of Sage.

"I enjoyed our conversation the other night," Sage offered, looking over to Michael.

"Me, too. Most people think shop talk should be left at work. But my work is who I am. I love talking about it."

Sage told Michael that MJ had said love was an important part of the job. "It seemed a strange thing to say when I first heard it," Sage said.

"She says a lot of things that seem strange at first," Michael said. "Has she told you about the Three Levels of Interaction yet?"

"She mentioned them the other night," Sage said. "We were talking about a guy named Frank who'd been a real bugger during a mediation she was facilitating. She told me Frank had been operating at Level One and that she had to reframe the discussion to get him to function on a different level. We're supposed to talk about the different levels the next time we get together."

"I'd never heard of the Three Levels of Interaction," Michael said, "before she introduced them to me. It made perfect sense once she explained them." He paused. "You do know they're her brain child, don't you?"

"I wasn't aware of that," Sage answered.

"That's why I hadn't heard of them before," he said chuckling. "So Frank was a Level One?"

The waitress returned with Sage's order. When she left, Michael continued, "Did she get Frank to move to another Level?"

"She did," Sage answered.

"The way she does that is something, isn't it?" he asked.

"I'd never seen anything like it," Sage said. "It was incredible. If I hadn't seen it with my own eyes, I don't think I would have believed it. Frank was in no mood to work through anything. But by the time it was all over, Frank was helping solve everyone else's problems."

"Good for you," Michael said. "You've witnessed an evolution in modern mediation. You said she was going to explain the different levels. I'm assuming you haven't learned what they are yet?"

"Not yet," said Sage. "MJ merely mentioned them. She said she would explain them in detail when we had more time.

"She identified the Three Levels of Interaction years ago and has been using them ever since, "Michael said. "She enlightened me, and I get amazing results whenever I use them. Frank was at Level One, and that's where a lot of people start. I used to get so frustrated trying to get people like him to move from conflict to compromise. That is, from Level One to Level Two," he told Sage.

"Level Two?"

"Yes," Michael answered. "Level Two is compromise. It's a rather wrong-headed, everybody-wins, conciliation paradigm I was caught up in like everyone else. So, yeah, I kept trying to get people like Frank to compromise and kept getting lousy results. Oh, I thought I was doing great at the time, but I know better now."

Sage took a bite of bread and a sip of her latté. "What exactly is Level One?" she asked. "I know you don't want to steal MJ's thunder, but maybe you could borrow a little of it. Just this once."

"I don't think she'd really care anyway," Michael said, shrugging. "Okay, look. Level One Interactions represent a minimal investment in thought and always result in conflict. They're actually monologues disguised as dialogues. Level One Interactions reinforce the notion that nobody is as smart as you are. It allows people to exclude the ideas of others or to open themselves to diverse thinking. As you might guess, alienation is predictable. One or both sides engage in a one-sided discussion that doesn't involve listening to the opposition. Even though each of them hears what the other is saying, neither is actually paying attention."

"Active Intelligent Listening?" Sage asked. "That's what you're talking about, right?"

"You sure you're not playing me?" Michael asked, smiling.

"Of course not," Sage said. "MJ explained it in an earlier conversation."

"Cool," Michael said. "Now where was I?"

"Level One," Sage reminded him.

"Yes, of course," Michael said, "Level One Interactions involve a low-level thought process that is entirely self-centered and controlling. It's destructive. It pushes both sides toward confrontation. Taken to the extreme, Level One interactions can end violently. It's all-out war without the weapons…well, sometimes with the weapons."

Sage nodded and took another sip of her latté. "You mean like when a union wants a pay increase and the administration claims to not have the money."

"Exactly," Michael agreed. "An argument like that, especially when it involves money, can last for years."

"That's where we come in," Sage told Michael while motioning for him to go on.

"Thank goodness for union disputes," Michael joked. "How about this? Ever heard of an employee who made a suggestion only to have it summarily dismissed by a supervisor?" Michael didn't wait for an answer; he pushed right on. There was a touch of sarcasm in his tone. "Or, how many times has someone asked for your input and then helpfully and immediately given you a thousand reasons why your idea wouldn't work."

"Every other week," Sage said with a smirk.

"How do you think employees on the wrong end of such a rejection feel?" Michael asked. "Do you think they're like, 'Wow, that's great, you didn't listen to a word I said!'"

"I've been there," Sage said. "I can tell you exactly how it feels. Suffice it to say, I wasn't jumping up and down to offer any more suggestions."

"Of course you weren't," Michael said. "And you're a reasonable person. But what happens when the person who's rejected is less reasonable? Most of the time they just go back to work. But sometimes they feel compelled to argue the point. When that happens, it rarely ends well for the employee."

Sage interrupted. "I had a friend who was fired because he tried to tell his supervisor that the agency was about to violate the patient confidentiality law. He recommended a different protocol. His boss went ballistic and demanded the information be released anyway. My friend explained he could lose his license for providing the records as ordered. His boss said, 'Fine. Don't worry about your license. You don't have a job. You're fired.'"

"A classic Level One Interaction," Michael said. "And a perfect example of how destructive Level One can be. It always ends badly, but it doesn't always end peacefully. Employees have been known to throw things or even to punch a supervisor during such an encounter. Worst case, an employee leaves then comes back with an AK to shoot the place up."

"That's why so many companies now have workplace violence policies in place," Sage suggested ruefully.

"Hundreds, thousands, maybe even millions of interactions take place every day on Level One," Michael said. "An angry airline passenger, a case of road rage, or an aggressive sibling rivalry. Did you know that most domestics start as a simple argument? Family quarrels are no different than any other Level One interaction. If either person views the argument as a force of wills, he or she is likely to react by meeting force with like force or greater force. If one or the other raises his or her voice, the opponent is likely to reciprocate. One person gets loud, and the other responds by talking louder, possibly even shouting. The process usually continues until one side 'wins' or at least thinks they've won."

"I know things can get physical when a person feels they're losing control," Sage said. "If I can't win the argument intellectually, I'll beat you into submission."

"That's Level One in a nutshell," Michael said. "It's a one-dimensional thought process. One party starts out with an extreme position while the other side is unwilling to accept it. If one side is willing to force his or her position by any means, you'll generally get an equally aggressive reaction from the other side."

"So," Sage interjected, "Level One interactions always move the discussion toward confrontation. That is what you're saying, right?"

"Absolutely," Michael answered. "People committed to Level One think on a one-dimensional plane, moving inevitably toward a destructive culmination on a unidirectional continuum." He smiled. "I got that from MJ," he said. "Pretty heady stuff, huh?"

"Sounds like rocket science for mediators," Sage quipped with a smile.

"Anyway," Michael offered, "MJ would say that at this level you take a contentious circumstance, add a confrontational response, and you get an out-of-control solution."

"People on the first level only think in one direction," Sage said. "It's about winning at any cost. They'll do whatever it takes. I get it."

"That's right," Michael agreed. "We've both seen it just like everyone else on the planet. It can start out simply enough. It's like when you go to an auction and find something you really want. You figure you'll bid a certain amount because that's what it's worth to you.

Then the bidding starts. And there's some guy who won't stop bidding against you. You bid, then he ups the bid. You bid again, and he ups it again. The next thing you know, you've gone way over what you said you'd pay. But you'll be damned if you'll let that guy go home with your prize. I call it the 'auctioneering syndrome.' You bid until you win. You also end up paying way more than you intended. So, did you win or did you lose? One of you didn't win the bid, and the other paid way more than the item was worth. But the *win* was the important thing. That's Level One. You may get what you want, but at what price?"

"That's like some arguments I've had with my husband," Sage said. "There have been times I'd forgotten why we were arguing in the first place. And even though I didn't want to fight anymore, I couldn't make myself stop. That ever happen to you?" she asked, a little sheepishly.

Michael responded, "Are you kidding? I think it happens to everyone. I can't count the number of times I've been in a situation where I should have stopped talking and didn't.

"This type of interaction happens a lot in arbitrations. Being in mediation confers a certain amount of authority to the participants," Michael continued. "That leads some people to believe that just being in the room gives them a special authority to control the session. Have you ever seen a subordinate go after a supervisor in one of your sessions?"

Sage nodded. She'd seen it way too often.

"They forget the boss is still the boss," Michael continued. "They act as if they've been anointed with some special power to force their position. Interpersonal communication stemming from that kind of thinking is likely to lead to a destructive outcome."

Sage noticed Michael had suddenly gotten an odd look on his face. "Something wrong?" she asked.

"Not really," he replied. "It's just that this can get confusing. Power is a funny thing. If you have too much, it can be a problem. But not having enough is a problem, too. In reality it's more about the power you *think* you have than the power you actually possess. A person who thinks he's all-powerful and one who believes he or she has no power at all can react in much the same way."

"How so?" Sage asked.

"Well," Michael explained, "both will push to reinforce or improve their position. To get the upper hand, most people will use their position, expertise, charisma, or they'll bully or try to entice the opposition. It doesn't matter how much power a person has. If they perceive they're losing, they'll raise the stakes."

"Now you're generalizing," Sage said. "That doesn't happen all the time. People don't always behave like that."

"It does in *Level One* encounters," Michael said. "Unless both parties move to another level, the stakes will be raised, and somebody will lose. Depending on the nature of the interaction, the person in the less influential position may resort to force to win. At the same time, a person who believes he or she has absolute control or influence may escalate the situation just to reinforce his or her sense of omnipotence."

"I don't understand what you mean when you use the terms 'less influential' or 'absolute influence,'" Sage said.

"Remember I told you that a person's actual power was not what determines how he or she would respond? It's the *perception* of power that dictates the reaction. Having a perception of too much control can be just as volatile as believing you've lost control. The reactions can be identical. This can be either to prove that one is in fact 'all powerful' or to attempt not to be thought of as 'impotent.' If the force used is challenged, a person may increase the level and/or type of coercion to maintain the upper hand."

"Give me an example," Sage said.

"Okay. Let's look at the police. The police are trained to take and maintain control of any situation. Unfortunately, not everyone they encounter is prepared to comply with an officer's instructions. Understanding this, the police are taught to meet force with like force or greater force."

Sage shuffled in her seat. "I can see what's coming."

"I'm sure you can," Michael replied. "What happens next is a natural consequence of mirroring another's behavior and/or upping the stakes. If the suspect raises his or her voice, the officer is apt to raise his voice in response.

If that person continues, the officer will escalate his response to maintain control. The officer may get louder or resort to barking orders. If the suspect still doesn't comply, the officer may use a physical restraint and get increasingly more aggressive until he or she achieves absolute compliance."

"That's fascinating," Sage opined. "The continuum you're talking about, by its very nature, is a prescription for escalation. It can't help but cause a discussion to become increasingly more aggressive. It encourages confrontation."

Michael nodded in agreement and said, "And it happens every day in a thousand different ways. You ever watch two children argue over something as simple as a toy? They start yelling at each other and invariably one of them pushes the other. It's the same use of force continuum the police use. Everybody at some point, either wittingly or unwittingly, will increase the amount of pressure or force they use to get what they want. We are better served if we simply acknowledge that control is an illusion, and absolute control is beyond illusion. Some people *are* naturally pugnacious and insist on either winning or losing. Whenever there's a power imbalance, whether it's real or not, conflict will often be the result."

"It's my experience," Sage said, "that few people really want to fight. Most people, given a chance, will embrace compromise to avoid conflict."

"That's right," Michael said. "Everybody I know will tell you total disagreement and zero-sum confrontations are undesirable. Solutions engineered through confrontation won't last. Understanding however, engenders cooperation and commitment. When people understand the opposing perspective, they become significantly more agreeable to finding solutions where no one has to lose. That's what happened with Frank. He was given an honorable way out, an opportunity to win where no one else would have to lose, and he took it. But how to achieve this kind of understanding is a long discussion we should probably reserve for another day."

Sage was looking at Michael with a puzzled expression. "Is there ever a circumstance where Level One Interactions are appropriate?" she asked.

"Of course," Michael replied. "Football, baseball, golf, tennis! Any athletic competition is an example of healthy Level One Interactions. Lawyers in litigation, a debate team, or a game of chess all fall into this category. They have winners and losers, unless there's a tie. But even in civilized contests like these, the potential for physical violence still exists. It's not uncommon to see things take a turn when a power imbalance becomes part of the equation. Look at what can happen when one team starts walloping the other. Tempers flare, and the battle begins. Almost a guarantee in hockey. Either side can start it, the all-powerful or the impotent."

Taking the last bite of her bread, Sage, feeling kind of full, and not merely of cake and coffee, told Michael it was time she got on with *Sidewalk Days*. She thanked him for the talk and started to leave some money on the table to pay for her snack.

"What's this?" Michael asked pointing to the money. "I invited you. Your money's no good here."

"You sure?" Sage asked.

"Of course," Michael responded. "You can get the next one," he said, smiling with a tip of his head. "Besides, you may need it. Some of these sale prices are higher than the MSRP."

Sage got a funny look on her face. "The Manufacturer's Suggested Retail Price," Michael said, shaking his head.

Sage laughed. "Have a good day, Michael!" she called out as she moved away from the table and ambled through the throng of people ogling the various wares.

Level I

Level I interactions are emotionally confrontational and destructive by nature. These interactions take a contentious circumstance, add a confrontational response resulting in out-of-control solutions.

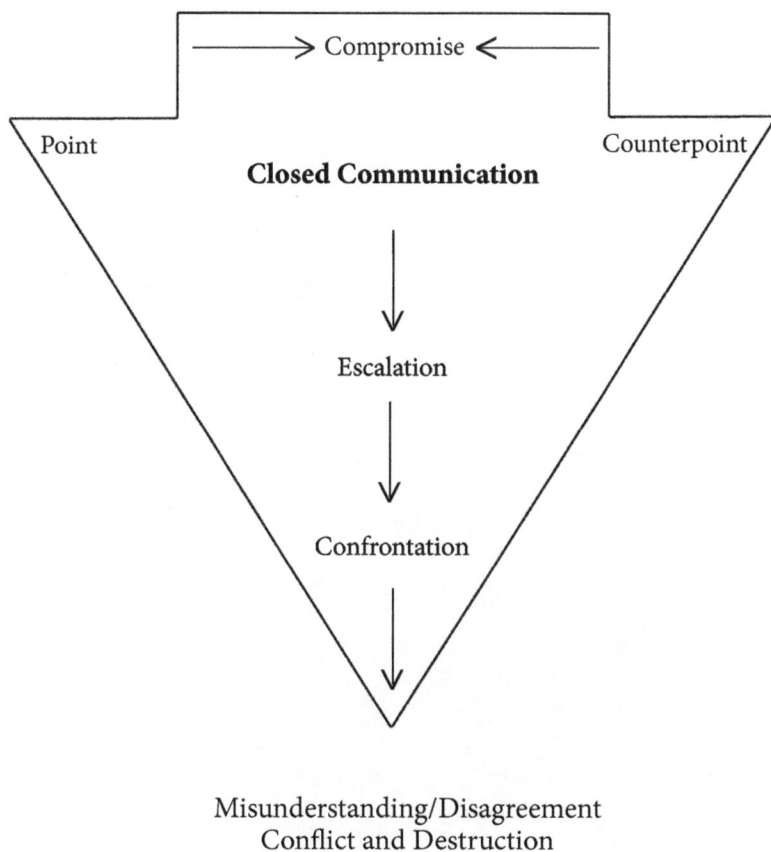

```
        ┌──────→ Compromise ←──────┐
        │                          │
  Point │                          │ Counterpoint
        Closed Communication
                  │
                  ↓
             Escalation
                  │
                  ↓
            Confrontation
                  │
                  ↓
```

Misunderstanding/Disagreement
Conflict and Destruction

8

Compromise: Level II Interactions

"Michael is right," MJ exclaimed. "Sometimes people get locked into a position and are just plain unwilling to see any other option. That's when you'll need to decide how to proceed. Do you keep trying for a different level, continue the row, or walk away?"

"But isn't getting people to move from conflict to a more favorable position the whole point?" Sage asked.

"It is. But what if they just won't budge?" MJ said.

Sage shrugged and said, "You keep trying?"

"Not necessarily," MJ said. "Sometimes you'll need to accept the fact that not everyone is willing to alter their thinking. If they lock it up on Level One…well, that's it. It's either annihilate the opposition or walk away."

"Where's the good in that?" Sage asked.

"There isn't any," MJ said. "That's the nature of Level One Interactions. They're pretty unhelpful. If either party refuses to budge, one of them is apt to win, albeit at the expense of the other. And make no mistake about it, some people just want to fight. When you run into one of those, you should recognize the futility in attempting to communicate at a higher level. If either party sets up shop at Level One, then Level One is *de facto* the level of interaction, full stop. It doesn't matter which level the other side is attempting to work from."

"*You* seem to be able to get people to cooperate," Sage said.

"That's because most people prefer to avoid conflict," MJ continued. "I use a person's propensity for avoidance to my advantage. I look for ways to provide an adversary with an honorable way out. And time is a wonderful equalizer. Used appropriately it can ease the effects of anger and enhance the prospects for empathy. Of course, the reverse can also happen. Unfortunately, the easiest way to avoid conflict is to compromise. And that's to my disadvantage.

"Avoiding conflict is why compromise is so appealing. That, and the fact that we've been taught to compromise since we learned to walk. It's been forced down our throats like a bad pill. Nobody really likes it, but everybody does it."

"You've told me a couple of times now that compromise means letting go of something you'd rather keep. And that finding ways to compromise is more difficult than duking it out. Why not just put the gloves on and get at it?" asked Sage.

"That is happening a lot more these days," MJ replied. "Conflict can be ugly. The results can be ugly as well. But compromise...well, compromise lets us pretend we're cooperating. We tell ourselves we're trying to find common ground. But it's an illusion. It's an illusion we're content to indulge, but nevertheless, an illusion. We convince ourselves that if we compromise, everybody wins. How many times have you heard that?" MJ asked.

Sage shook her head, "I don't know. Hundreds if not thousands."

MJ nodded. "It's not true. Actually, everybody loses when they compromise. It's a Level Two Interaction. It's less confrontational than standing toe to toe. But it's still a contentious endeavor. It leads neither to understanding nor to outright confrontation. It merely leads to appeasement. Really, it's nothing more than a marginal way to mollify our acceptance of less. It leaves both sides feeling a sense of loss and subsequently dissatisfied."

"Why do people do it then?" Sage asked.

"We convince ourselves that losing for the sake of getting along is acceptable. Compromise is not entirely destructive, but it's not all that constructive either. It's just a middle-of-the-road exercise that leads to placation."

"Look here," MJ said, placing her hands over her chest with her fingers extended and touching. "Level Two thought processes tend to be linear. Each side moves to the left or right of the position from which they started."

Then she slowly pulled her hands apart in a straight line to either side of her body. "They neither engage in combat nor seek to understand. Movement up toward understanding or down toward conflict is minimized. What movement there is merely influences how agreeable or disagreeable the discussion is. People are pulled either to the left or to the right of the extremes. This results in relatively linear reconciliations."

Putting her hands down, she shook her head, pressing her lips together at the sides of her mouth. She continued, "This level of discussion is predicated on conciliation and acceptable loss. We've used this level of thought forever, and the results are always the same: Mutual dissatisfaction. That's because we make agreements where neither side wins.

"Negotiations are a case in point. Many negotiations begin in conflict and only later move to compromise or settlement. Rarely do they move to understanding or consensus. Unfortunately, many never evolve beyond confrontation. Even when there's an opportunity to compromise, some people would rather be contentious."

Sage smiled. "I know exactly what you're talking about. I worked a mediation where the union voted to reject a pay increase of almost 40 percent. They had been dueling with management for three years. A new administrator took over and found the union employees were grossly underpaid. He proposed a huge pay increase. He also discovered some issues within the management rights clause of the contract. He offered the union a 40 percent raise and proposed a couple minor language changes. The union immediately rejected the offer.

"I didn't understand at the time, but I get it now. The union had only asked for a 5 percent pay increase. Crazy as it may sound, they rejected an increase of almost 40 percent. They blamed it on the language. They didn't care about the language. They got caught up in the 'auctioneering syndrome,' and wanted to one-up management at every turn."

Sage leaned back in her seat. "After a long hard-fought battle, the union reluctantly agreed to accept the language management wanted. It passed by one vote. I couldn't believe it—one vote. Even though they got way more money than they'd have gotten otherwise, half the membership wasn't even close to happy. The process strained the union/management relationship almost beyond repair, and for no good reason."

"Was it Michael who told you about the 'auctioneering syndrome'?" MJ asked.

"Yes," Sage said, "he mentioned it when I saw him at *Sidewalk Days*. He said some people have an inability to let themselves win. That's crazy. Why do we do that?"

"I got nothing," MJ said.

"That's exactly what happened to this group," Sage said. "They'd begun the negotiation intending from the start to go to arbitration. That was how they thought they'd win. They got so caught up in trying to get to arbitration, they were oblivious to the fact that their adversary wasn't being adversarial. They eventually took the raise, but many in the group were unhappy because they hadn't gone to arbitration. In their eyes, they hadn't won. They were undoubtedly much better off, but they were hung up on not getting what they originally wanted. *Only* arbitration would be *winning."*

"The interaction you just described ended like far too many Level Two Interactions I've dealt with over the years," MJ said. "The problem with Level Two Interactions is that when you take a contentious circumstance and add a little rationality to an otherwise conciliatory response, you end up with an appeasement. Acquiescence tends to feel like self-abasement. Yet people tend to embrace compromise as if it were a good thing. In most circles, it's the preferred way to resolve disputes. I find it peculiar that so many people who extol the virtues of compromise wouldn't for a minute entertain the concept when it comes to issues of principle, of family, politics, or religion. Remember our discussion with Michael?"

"Yeah, I do," Sage recalled. "He made it pretty clear that the only thing you should compromise is something you care nothing about."

"Is there something wrong with that mindset, or is it just me?" MJ asked.

"That's why I'm here," Sage said. "Our willingness to embrace this kind of thinking has been bugging me for years. And no, it's not just you."

"People rarely compromise without getting bruised feelings or some sense of having sold out," MJ proclaimed. "I'd bet some of the smartest people you know have told you, 'You know you've brokered a good deal when no one at the table is happy.' Am I right?"

"Yup, heard it a thousand times," Sage answered, chuckling. "Why hasn't the rest of the world figured this out yet?"

MJ scrunched up her brow. "I haven't a clue. By their own admission, compromise is nothing more than a concerted effort to make the other side unhappy. And the masses are okay with that. It's a lose/lose proposition. Nobody wins. It's silly. Why would anyone spend their time doing everything in their power to make everyone around them unhappy, including themselves? That's absolutely absurd!"

"I can't wait to see how things go at tomorrow's meeting," Sage said.

"They'll likely go much as you expect," MJ offered. "But then again, maybe not."

"I'm expecting a lot," said Sage. "I'm looking for another miraculous outcome. Like the day we first met."

"After tomorrow I pray you won't see such outcomes as miraculous," MJ said. "I hope you'll see them more as the result of calculated reasoning and a commitment to understanding. Remember the adage, 'You reap what you sow'? Well, it's true. Ultimately, you get what you give. It's as simple or as complicated as that." MJ smiled, and Sage smiled back.

"I still can't wait until tomorrow," Sage said, preparing to leave.

"Me neither," MJ told her. "Me neither."

Level II

Level II communications are linear in nature with minimal movement towards either more open or closed interactions. Compromise is a middle-of-the-road exercise that takes a contentious circumstance, adds a conciliatory response resulting in appeasement.

Open Communication

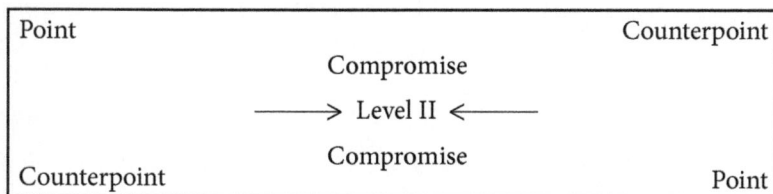

Point	Counterpoint
	Compromise
	⟶ Level II ⟵
	Compromise
Counterpoint	Point

Closed Communication

9

Empathetic Understanding: Level III Interactions

The meeting didn't last long. People left the room giving each other high fives, low fives, and congratulatory hugs. It was boisterous. Everyone was celebrating, except Frank. Frank just sat at the table, smiling. A couple of people walked over and thanked him for the work he'd done.

"This worked out just fine, didn't it?" he said.

"Yes, it did," they agreed. They patted Frank on the back and filed out of the room.

MJ was packing her things and thanking people as they left. "Is something wrong, Frank?" she asked.

"No," he replied. "Just the opposite. I'd expected this mediation to go on for weeks and end with me being upset for the next six months. Instead, it lasted for a couple of days, and I got everything I wanted. Everybody else seems happy, too. I can't remember how many of these I've done, and this is a first," he said, grinning from ear to ear. He looked at MJ for a moment. "How'd you *do* that?"

"I didn't do anything. You did," she said. "You all did."

"Not without you we didn't," Frank told her. "I've worked with these same people for years, and we've never gotten along, not like this. And we damned sure never walked away glad-handing and patting each other on the back!"

He paused, apparently considering what had just taken place. "Three sessions," he said. "That's all it took. I just wanted to say thank you."

"Well, you're welcome."

"What's your secret?" Frank inquired.

MJ smiled. "Why does everybody think I have a secret?"

"If it wasn't a secret, everybody'd be doing it," Frank said. "And they're not. So, it has to be a secret."

"You really want to know?"

"Do fish swim?" Frank answered. "Maybe you could show me how to do it, too."

"Do you have a few minutes?" MJ asked looking to Sage for a response.

"I'm as curious as he is," Sage said, gesturing toward Frank. "Count me in."

"May I take notes?" Frank asked. "I don't want to forget anything. I've got a great memory, but it's a little short." He laughed at his own joke.

"If you like," MJ said. "But simply writing it down won't help much. You've got to be willing to live it."

"And you've got to *put some love into it*," Sage chimed in. She was looking at Frank but immediately shifted her attention to MJ, who was smiling and nodding, her auburn hair swaying like a child's swing in a breeze.

"You certainly do," MJ answered, still nodding her approval.

"I gotta do what?" Frank asked in a voice an octave higher than normal.

"Love, Frank," MJ said. "That's one of the things you need to do—to get people to buy into what you're selling. It's a little hard to wrap your head around at first. But Sage is right. You need to have an affinity for what you do and who you're doing it with to get the best results. Then you've gotta open your mind and let go of what you *think* you know in favor of what you may come to know."

Frank listened intently, nodding therapeutically to make sure MJ knew he was engaged. Sage settled in as MJ made her way to the white board. She picked up a marker and drew an elongated diamond. "Level One," she wrote at the base of the diagram. At the midpoint she wrote, "Level Two," and at the top, "Level Three."

"People interact on three different levels," MJ said. "Whether you're conscious of it or not, you're always functioning at one level or another. Level One is conflict," she pointed to the bottom of the diagram. Moving her hand up the diagram she said, "Level Two is compromise, and Level Three is empathetic understanding. The Third Level is, at least in part, a synthesis of differing ideas and emotional attachments."

She faced Frank. "Now, which level do you think you were on the first day you walked in that door?" She motioned to the open door.

Frank winced. "You want me to answer that?"

"Of course I do," MJ replied.

Sage raised her hand, "I know, I know!" she said, raising her hand and waving it back and forth like a six-year-old at the back of a classroom.

Frank squinted his eyes at Sage. "Level One?" he suggested without much enthusiasm. Sage was still waving her hand. Frank knew she was goading him.

"Was that a question or an answer?" MJ asked.

"That was me shamefully acknowledging I was all the way wrong," Frank said. "I hate to admit it, but when I first walked in I was ready for battle. I wasn't the only one though. Everybody else was up for it, too."

"Didn't you think about compromising?" Sage inquired. "I mean, didn't you think when the smoke cleared, you'd end up compromising anyway?"

"No," Frank said without hesitating. "I was tired of compromising. I wanted to go nuclear and blow 'em completely out of the water."

"So, why didn't you?" MJ asked.

"You didn't let me," Frank said, and he started laughing. "You got me to start talking about what I needed from the group. Before I knew it, the session was over. Then at the second session, when I tried to put on my boxing gloves, you stopped me before I could lace 'em up."

"Why do you think that was?" MJ prodded.

"I'm not sure."

"Okay," MJ began. "You were upset when you first got here. It was obvious to everyone in the room. You pretty much let us know you were ready for World War III. So instead of indulging you, I asked you to explain your position. I simply asked you to tell us your story."

"My story?" Frank asked.

"Yes, Frank, your *story*. You needed the people in this room to know how you felt and why you felt that way. I merely provided you with an opportunity to tell them. So how did that make you feel?"

Frank thought about it for a moment. "I felt relieved," he said. "Now that I think about it, I felt relieved. I didn't think anything would come of it, but at least I put it out there. I wasn't sure if anyone would actually listen, but I said what I needed to say."

"People did listen though, didn't they?" MJ added.

"I was listening," Sage said.

"I learned quite a bit as well," MJ added. "I wanted you to know that I did hear you. I wanted you to know that everyone in the room had heard you. That's why I asked if anyone remembered you telling us anything different. And no one did."

Frank interrupted. "That took me by surprise. I hadn't thought anyone was paying attention. I was really taken aback when you asked the other side how *they* could help me get what I needed without having to compromise. And they did it. They actually did it!"

"So, then what did *you* do?" MJ asked.

"Well, I couldn't let them come up with better answers than I had. So I started thinking of what I could do to solve the problem myself. Of course, you'd told me I needed to come up with answers that didn't force them to compromise either. Next thing I knew, we were working together. We did what we needed to fix the problem without either side having to compromise their position." Frank thought for a moment. "It was kind of cool."

"It was, wasn't it," MJ said. "You see, Frank, I needed you to know that you didn't have to accept the way things had been. You did have alternatives. The best way to achieve favorable outcomes, in disputes such as this, is to demonstrate that it's entirely possible to engage in constructive dialogue where losing is not an option. So I introduced you to the Third Level of Interaction. That is 'empathetic understanding.'" MJ wrote the phrase on the white board at the top of the diagram.

She pointed her finger at it. "Level Three Interactions," she said, "are the antithesis of Level One. They're complete opposites. They also transcend interactions on Level Two because empathy is required. Level Three is about getting people to *see* alternative points of view. It's a legitimate dialogue where people talk *with* each other, not *at* one another."

MJ walked over and sat next to Frank. She gestured back and forth between them. "Interacting at Level Three," she said, "is evolutionary. Instead of 'us versus them', there is no them, it's just us. It's people working as advocates, not adversaries, allowing them to synthesize divergent ideas." She got up and went back to the board.

"Okay," Frank said. "Let me see if I've got this. We all need to work to understand each other better. And we do that by listening to and empathizing with other people's points of view. Understanding and feeling where the other side is coming from will likely alter the interaction. That way finding a resolution to what would otherwise be a dispute becomes a group exercise?"

"Correct. Do that and you'll have no need to push back," MJ added. "There will be no need to pressure others nor to feel pressured. You won't need to sacrifice or give anything away that you really don't want to. Anything given will be because it's best for everyone involved. And you'll give it freely." MJ had stopped writing and was directing Sage and Frank's attention to the board.

"You already know that Level One is conflict," MJ told them. "It's a zero-sum game. I win. You lose. I think we've also established that compromising anything of consequence isn't something anybody really wants, likes, or should do either. The reason is simple. Everybody loses. You surrender something important to you. I surrender something important to me. It's a lose/lose scenario.

"Level Three on the other hand offers us a chance to be better. It affords everybody an opportunity to win." Again she pointed to the board. "There are five 'pillars' to effective Level Three Interactions."

"First," she said, "**Let them tell their story**. Everybody has one, and they'll want you to hear it. Listening to the other side's story sets the stage for open and productive discussions."

"That's what you did with Frank," Sage acknowledged. "But nobody else told *their* story. Why didn't you have everybody tell their stories?"

"Nobody else seemed to need to," MJ answered. "If they had, I would have given them an opportunity as well. But only once," she added. "You only get to tell your story once."

"Why only once?" Sage inquired.

"People want their story heard," MJ offered. "And they'll tell it over and over, and over again if you let them. As people provide differing accounts it can become a contest. With each telling, the tales tend to grow. You'll never get to the issues if all you do is listen to the stories."

A small groan leaked from Sage's mouth. "I hadn't thought of that."

"That's a good point," Frank interjected. "I'd have told mine again for sure. It's easy to get wound up. If someone had pulled on that door even a little, I'd have been off to the races. I'm embarrassed to admit it, but that's what would have happened."

"Moving on," MJ said. "The second pillar is to **agree to mutually acceptable objectives**. You've got to find a commonality and unify your purpose. Develop or reframe mutually acceptable goals and objectives using legitimate, verifiable information. 'Common' and 'mutually acceptable' are important terms to remember. When the agreed upon objectives are met, the results must satisfy the needs of everyone affected. Everybody has to feel the win."

Frank gave Sage a knowing look as they listened. They'd bypassed step number two after MJ recited Frank's story. Everyone was so excited to get started, they began offering ideas immediately after MJ completed the recounting. MJ probably figured it would be more productive for them to continue rather than interrupt the flow. After all, she'd had them establish their objectives later in the session.

"Three," MJ continued. "**Empowerment**. Everyone involved should be comfortable. Discussions must be open, honest, and direct without fear of reprisal or domination. Mitigate any power imbalances. An imbalance of power will skew the results of any outcome."

"I can't emphasize this point enough," MJ said. "Power can be a terribly corrupting influence. And any significant power imbalance can lead to conflict in a heartbeat. Conflict and confrontation are right around the corner if you don't effectively empower everyone involved. Achieving balance is key." MJ slowed to see if her companions were with her.

They were. So, she smiled, then continued with the list. "Pillar number four is **Active Intelligent Listening**. Don't just listen to what's being said. You must look for nonverbal expressions that provide color, clarity, and conscience to the conversation."

"Excuse me," Frank said. "I need you to elaborate."

"No problem," MJ replied looking in Sage's direction. "Would you care to do the honors?"

"Sure," Sage said. "The idea is to listen discriminatingly, for inflection, for tone, and use your eyes to observe body language and physical signs of stress, emotion, or resolve. In other words, you need to listen with all of your senses, giving the person speaking your full attention."

"Good job," MJ offered. "Alright then, let's finish this. The last of the pillars is to **provide an honorable out**. If someone is married to a position and is likely to lose face if they change their stance, give them an honorable way out."

"That's what you did by getting the other side to help me find a way to get what I needed without making me compromise," Frank said, "isn't it? Then you did the same thing with me by getting me to look for ways I could help *them*. That's pretty clever."

MJ looked at Frank, at Sage, then back to Frank again. "You did all the work. I merely facilitated."

She went on, saying, "Level Three Interactions seek understanding. Understanding generates empathy, and empathy gets you to the most viable responsive solutions. Level Three Interactions are what you might call 'selfless' commitments to doing what's good and right. People start thinking of what's good for the 'other person.' And the whole interaction changes. They take the best available information and harmonize any divergent ideas or concepts."

Frank quickly slipped in. "So, people at Level Two feel compelled to compromise, to sacrifice something important to them and then expect an equal or greater sacrifice from the other side. However, you're saying at this third level, you rise above that?"

"Correct," MJ answered. "If followed to their conclusion, either compromise or empathetic understanding could render a similar result. In compromise each party will have begrudgingly given something up. However, with empathetic understanding nothing is lost or sacrificed. At Level Three decisions are taken willingly, without remorse, because they're what's best for everyone involved."

"No more knocking each other around?"

"Right again," she said. "Nothing is sacrificed. It breaks down like this. Level Three Interactions approach a contentious, confrontational circumstance and add a reasoned, rational, and inclusive response. Rationality and inclusion develop benevolently beneficial solutions. Lovely word, isn't it: 'benevolent.' It means 'kindly, wishing others well.' We can all do that, and in so doing, we transcend conflict."

"Intellectually, it's easy to see why Level Three Interactions are more complicated than Level One or Two. For one thing, they require more patience."

"Uh-huh," Sage said. "When you first told me I needed more patience, I was a little miffed. Now I see where you were going with that. You didn't mean patience as in not doing anything, but patience as in 'being still, while listening' until I really understood the other person's viewpoint."

"Exactly," MJ said. "I think you've got it. At the same time this is *three-dimensional* thinking. Not push-pull, as in 'what I get, you give up.' But instead rising above the confrontation to get a broader perspective. You both know what can happen when you get it right."

"This stuff is fascinating. It seems to have applications well beyond union negotiations and arbitrations," Frank added. "I'm going to use it on my sixteen-year-old."

"Sure. You can use it all the time," MJ replied. "That's a good segue to answering your earlier question about Active Intelligent Listening."

Sage stopped her. "You told me about Active Intelligent Listening when we were talking the other day."

"You and I talked about it. But Frank hasn't gotten it yet." MJ reminded her. "Active Intelligent Listening,

Frank, demands you commit to the process. You'll need to be open to changing your perspective. Unlike Level One or Two, the interaction at Level Three is not a contest. It's a collaboration. You can't talk over and around one another. Active Intelligent Listening doesn't allow for you to prepare what you believe to be your winning rebuff when you should be *paying attention.*"

"Guilty as charged!" Frank piped in. "But you have to admit, sometimes it's really hard to let people drone on when you already know what they're going to say."

"You mean when you *think* you know what they're going to say," Sage quipped. "I think that may be part of the problem MJ's describing. We don't really know what's about to be said, but we like to think we do. I'm guilty, myself. My husband is always telling me, 'That's not what I was going to say.' My bad."

MJ smiled beatifically. "Mine too. We all need to listen better. Any interaction will be more effective when done introspectively, that is, absorbing and assimilating what's being said. Active Intelligent Listening is not just hearing what's being said. It's watching for nonverbal indicators. It's deciphering a voice inflection, modulation or pitch. It's about reading body language. Do you have any idea what your body language was saying at the beginning of our first session, Frank?"

"Oh, yeah," Frank said. "It had to have been like looking at a brick wall. A brick wall with cannons on it."

"Well, what's it saying now?"

MJ and Sage both looked discerningly at Frank, sitting there, relaxed and comfortable.

"You've got me there. I look a lot more open I'm sure."

"Not open-*looking*, Frank. I would say you are more relaxed *because* you have in fact opened up. You're listening as well, actively listening."

"I'm trying to listen intelligently, too, but I'm about maxed out. This is a lot to take in."

All three laughed.

"You asked for it," MJ said.

"I did. So keep it coming."

"You sure?"

"Absolutely."

"What about you, Sage? Are you still with us?"

"Yes ma'am."

"Okay then. With Active Intelligent Listening you're compelled to stop, look, and listen so you truly understand empathetically. Empathy strengthens relationships and the *will* needed to cultivate mutually satisfying outcomes."

"Is that what you were doing when you had me tell my story?" Frank asked. "I'm thinking it was. Then you challenged the others to help me. But they had to do it without making me compromise or compromising themselves. That's brilliant. *Everything* about the interaction changed once you did that."

"You went from being adversaries to advocates," MJ said.

"And from being help*less* to help*ful*," Sage added. "How cool is that?"

"Pretty cool, I'd say," MJ offered. "You started thinking synergistically, absorbing and combining one another's ideas. That required you to open your minds and use an 'open-systems' approach. The group recognized that everyone and everything was interdependent. That means, nothing and no one could be isolated. Everyone had to focus on achieving *mutual* gains and interpersonal satisfaction."

MJ tapped her fingers on the top of her forehead and then on the top of the white board above the drawing. "Each of you had to start thinking on a higher level. That allowed the group to consider the breadth, depth, and scope of the issue, including the opposing perspective. That's what I mean by *three-dimensional* thinking."

"Outside the box," Sage declared.

"Way outside," Frank added.

"Unbeknownst to any of you," continued MJ, "that is, during the session anyway, Active Intelligent Listening became an essential component of the interaction. You had to listen to acquire understanding without the interfering prejudice of position. It helped you to develop a rapport that allowed for the melding of your ideas."

"Put like that," Sage offered, "Level Three exposes compromise for what it really is—a much lower-level interaction, requiring you to relinquish something you want to your disadvantage. But up here, at Level Three, neither side is expected to give up anything or to accept a loss."

"Right," MJ said. "Instead of settling, acquiescing, or pummeling each other, Level Three thinkers use Active Intelligent Listening to acquire a legitimate understanding of the issues. In order to gain an authentic understanding of the underlying contributors to the perceptions of another requires us to, one: **seek** for what motivates them to hold a particular perception; two: **separate** fact from fiction, that is, to help them distinguish what they really need from that which they merely think is necessary; and three: help **satisfy** their needs with the available resources—"

"Wait a minute!" Sage interjected before MJ could move on. "Can you do that again? Maybe you could write it down, so Frank and I can look at it more closely."

"What she said," Frank blurted quickly.

MJ obliged.

Use Active Intelligent Listening to
    1) Seek their motivations
    2) Separate fact from fiction
    3) Satisfy their actual needs

"Consider what happened with the 'Truth and Reconciliation Commission' in South Africa," MJ suggested. "While this analogy isn't as tidy as I'd like, I think it'll serve the purpose. Facing the prospect of certain violence, civil abuse, and oppression, the black and white communities, through the brilliant and compassionate leadership of

Nelson Mandela, managed to do the things Active Intelligent Listening contemplates. The people bared their motivations, behaviors and the consequences of their actions. The information was factual. And they, collectively, found a way to live together peacefully. The South African transition was peaceful when the world, including the majority of South Africans, predicted a bloodbath.

"Interacting in this way, whether on the large canvas of national or international affairs or a smaller one like our recent mediation, nothing is lost or given up. Instead, the condition is redefined without conflict or compromise."

"So, there you have it," MJ said, dusting her hands off, as if it was a 'done deal.' "I think we're finished."

Frank rubbed his chin, smiled, and shook his head. "I've been in the ring since before I can remember. And not once have I left a mediation, of any sort, feeling the way I do now. Even when I'd stomped the other side, I didn't feel this good. I'd have never guessed that giving without expectation and helping with no quid-pro-quo in mind could make me feel…so good. I'm free. 'Free at last, free at last, thank…'"

"Don't do that," MJ pleaded.

"Well, thank you anyway, Miss MJ."

"You ever think about teaching this stuff?" Sage asked.

"I just did!" MJ replied. They all laughed comfortably at that. Frank and Sage nodded to one another as MJ started picking up her things and motioned for Sage to join her.

"Well, I gotta get going, too," Frank said. "But I could kick this around all afternoon." Chuckling, he went on, "I think you've ruined me, MJ. How do I go back to kicking everybody's butt after this? What a world, what a world." Frank was mimicking the Wicked Witch of the West from the *Wizard of Oz*. "Well, have a good evening, ladies. It has been a pleasure."

"You, too," Sage said. MJ merely smiled.

And with that, Frank started down the hall and disappeared around a corner.

Empathetic Understanding

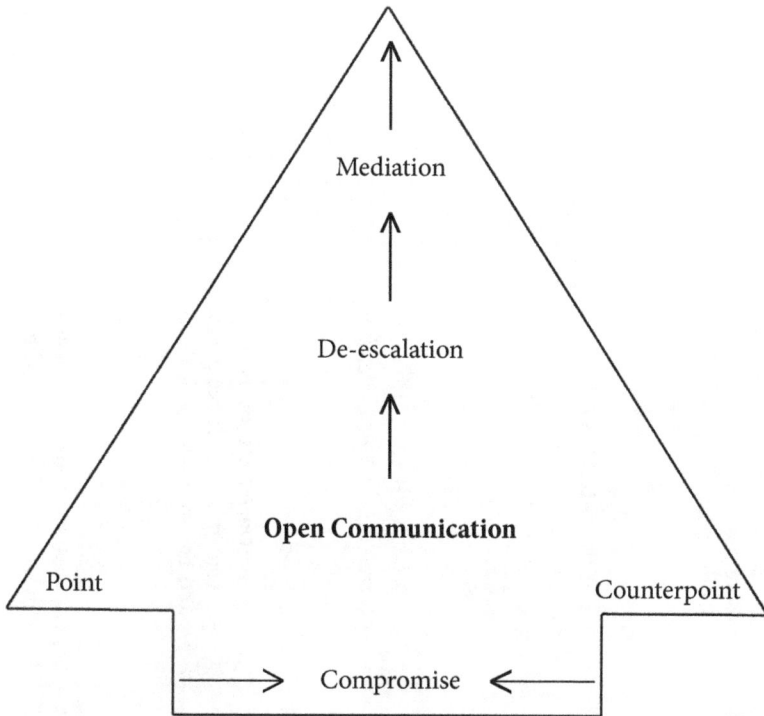

Mediation

De-escalation

Open Communication

Point

Counterpoint

Compromise

Level III Interactions synthesize divergent ideas. Level III Interactions take a contentious circumstance, adds a reasoned, responsive and inclusive response resulting in benevolently beneficial solutions.

Level III

Five Pillars to Empathetic Understanding

Balance the Power.
Ensure participants are on an equal footing with no fear of reprisal

Let them tell their story.
Participants need to be afforded an opportunity to be heard

Listen for substance.
(Active Intelligent Listening)

Agree on Objectives.
What are the perceived needs, how to proceed, and what is the desired outcome

Always leave a door open so others can save face if they need to.

10

The Three Ships of Success

Sage looked over her shoulder as Frank walked away. "He's in a very different place than when we started," she said.

"That's a good thing," MJ answered. "I have to remind myself constantly not to judge the book by its cover. Not everyone is able to accept the fact they need to change. Frank is a smart fellow. He is bright enough to adapt when it's to his advantage. Some people hold on even when they know they shouldn't. That's the difference between those who remain at Level One and those who transcend it and move to a higher level."

"Do people regress?" Sage asked. "I mean, once you've seen what success looks like at Level Three, how could you ever go back?"

"Don't forget," MJ said, "it's not always up to you to determine on which level you'll interact. The lowest level of interaction for either side is the *de facto* level of interaction for everyone involved. It's a version of the lowest common denominator."

"That's right," Sage said. "What was I thinking? Pretend I didn't ask that."

"Ask what?" MJ said, grinning. Sage chuckled.

Sage looked around, taking in what had turned out to be a beautiful day with a refreshing breeze. "I'm glad we decided to walk."

"Me too. Besides being out on such a gorgeous day and sharing good company, I can put a bow on the project we started when we first met."

Sage smiled again. "It seems like yesterday, and years ago at the same time," she said. "I've learned a lot. Like with Frank. He started out being pushy and got everyone up in arms. Then you got him to tell his story. Before I knew it, he was helping work through the difficult issues they all faced."

"That's the perfect lead-in to what I planned to share with you next," MJ told her.

"What's that?" Sage asked.

"Well," answered MJ, "The way you described Frank's development throughout the mediation, for one. Frank went from leading, albeit negatively, to following, and then to building relationships. It's what I call the *three ships of success—leadership, followership, and relationships.*"

"That's kind of catchy."

"Thanks," MJ responded. "I didn't have to think about it much. It just sort of happened. But back to the three ships. Frank started out by leading."

Sage screwed up her face, trying to recall how the meeting had kicked off. "That's not the way I remember it," she said. "It seems to me Frank started in a vitriolic tirade, which got everybody else going."

"You made my point," MJ told her. "Frank opened with his gloves on, and everybody else followed his lead. Unfortunately, the other people in the room took up the challenge at his level. The entire group unwittingly began interacting at the lowest possible level."

"I see what you're saying. Leadership isn't always positive," said Sage.

"As history unfortunately testifies," MJ agreed. "But we were able to reframe the discussion by encouraging Frank to tell his story. In doing so, he followed *my* lead."

"From leading to following," Sage offered.

"Exactly," MJ said. Then she went on, "The group followed my suggestion to help one another find solutions to their issues without forcing anyone to compromise. In the process, they fostered a new relationship."

Sage nodded, "The third ship just put into port."

"It did indeed," MJ acknowledged. "The more they helped one another the better it went. At some point, each of them led the discussion while they followed at others."

Sage knitted her brows together. "But you controlled the meeting," she said. "The group only did what you told them to do."

MJ shook her head, "I *controlled* nothing. I managed. I facilitated, that's all. I steered certain individuals into assuming the role of leader or follower as it served the overall interests of the group. I helped the group find ways to support each other. The harder they worked, the stronger the relationship became."

"Frank walked in adversarial. He didn't need anyone to help him with that," Sage said.

"No, he didn't," MJ agreed. "He took the lead in that all by himself. The group followed him into confrontation on their own as well. I didn't do a thing to instigate *that* process."

"That's how I saw it, too." Sage replied.

"All I did," MJ continued, "was assist in forming the dynamics of the interaction by assuming an early lead. Frank and the others willingly gave me that responsibility." MJ chuckled and began patting herself on the back. "That's what good facilitators do. And I'm *very* good!" Both women laughed at that.

MJ placed a hand on Sage's shoulder before resuming, "In every interpersonal interaction, someone will lead and someone will follow. Contrary to what some people would have you believe, there's no such thing as a leaderless interaction. Formally or informally, someone will lead, and someone will follow. Always and inevitably."

"That makes sense," Sage said. "I imagine a truly leaderless group would be an unfocused disaster."

"Too true," MJ acknowledged. "It's possible —actually it happens all the time— that the role of leader or follower may change several times during an interaction."

"How so?" Sage asked.

MJ gestured at their surroundings. "Why are we *walking* back to the office?"

"I don't know," Sage said, "because you suggested it?"

"Sure," MJ answered. "So, you're following my lead. But what if you had said, 'I don't want to walk, let's take a cab,' and I agreed? Who'd be leading then?"

"Me?" Sage asked.

"Of course," MJ said. "Remember, the leader or follower can change any number of times throughout the course of an interaction. What's important is that you understand the significance of being in the lead or following. What if we agreed to meet at a mutually acceptable place and one of us took a cab and the other walked, who's in the lead then?"

"I guess it depends on who suggested it," Sage replied. "But once we parted ways we'd be taking the lead for anything we did while separated. Wait—unless what we did had been planned before we parted ways. Wow."

"If you both agree to...I don't know...take the same steps or different modes of transportation, someone still had to broach the subject and someone had to accept the notion," MJ offered. "That happens. But even so, one person is still leading while the other is following." She looked at Sage and noticed that she looked uncertain. "Much of what determines who takes the lead depends on who has the most influence in the relationship. And that derives mostly from their perceptions of influence."

"How so?" Sage asked, "Can you elaborate?"

"Sure," MJ replied, "*Nema problema.*"

"What?"

"It means 'no problem,'" she said. "Something I picked up in my travels. It's about the only thing I can say in Serbo-Croatian. Well, that and 'good morning' or 'good afternoon.' But I digress. We were talking about the perception of influence."

"Yes," Sage said. "I'm not sure what you mean by that."

"Well," MJ explained, "people tend to give credence to others based on their perception of that person's potential to influence. For example, a person with a Ph.D. is likely to be perceived as more knowledgeable than someone without a degree. That perception is likely to be a factor in determining whether that person is viewed as a leader. There are many other characteristics that have the potential to influence as well. For instance, a person's charisma, status, or authority to grant a reward or impose a penalty. Each may contribute to any perception of that person as a potential leader."

"Are you saying that a person's social status is only as important as I perceive it to be?" Sage asked.

"Absolutely," MJ replied. "Your status as the president

of a small university may be significant to a person trying to get a degree there. But it may be of no consequence to a person who has a Master's Degree from an Ivy League institution."

"Okay," Sage said. "I get that."

"Likewise," MJ continued, "one person may find you compelling and intriguing while another may find you unattractive and boring. It's not so much what you have that matters. It's what others perceive you to have that makes the difference."

"I see," Sage said. "A leader has the ability to lead because those who follow them perceive they have good leadership characteristics. That's why some people who were great leaders in one circumstance fail in others."

"Right again," MJ said. "Leadership is situational. Every situation is different. The level of influence any one person has is dependent upon how those they seek to lead perceive them. The more characteristics a person is credited with, the greater his or her ability to influence will be."

"For instance," MJ said. "A highly respected police chief successfully led several major metropolitan police agencies for years. However, his leadership was met with disdain in the City of New York and he was forced to leave after a very short tenure. Coaches are another example. A coach can lead one team to great success while failing miserably with another. Some of football's best coaches have been fired because they couldn't get a team to the playoffs. Remember Herschel Walker? He was an amazing running back with the Cowboys but failed as a running back for the Vikings. His talent didn't change, but how he was perceived had."

Sage scratched at the side of her forehead. "I think I'm missing a couple of these traits."

"Perhaps," MJ said, "Use whatever you have to your advantage. The *judicious* use of influence engenders trust and respect. Few people gravitate to a leader who abuses his or her ability to influence."

"Like a dictator or a bully?" asked Sage.

"You're not wrong," MJ said, "But even dictators and bullies have followers. It's only when people trust and/or respect each other that they're likely to alternate between leading and following. Having said that, there are formal and informal leaders. The formal leader gets his or her authority by decree. The informal leader gets his or her authority from the people who choose to follow them. With friends, one generally defers to the other informally. In business, it's usually by edict or executive order. But an informal leader can override the influence of a formal leader."

Sage cocked her head to one side. "An 'informal' leader can override the directions of his boss? Really?"

"Sure," MJ answered. "Happens all the time, albeit to the chagrin of the person who's supposed to be in charge."

"I'm not getting it," Sage said, looking totally confused.

"Of course you are," MJ replied. "Who's in charge when you're conducting a mediation?"

"I am," Sage answered.

"And what about when you don't get the solution you hoped for?"

"I'm still in charge," Sage said.

"Perhaps formally," MJ answered. "But someone else actually lead the mediation if the outcome ended up being something other than you intended. An informal usurper undermined your ability to manage effectively." She paused for a moment before continuing. "Do you want something to drink?"

"No, I'm good," Sage responded.

"I think I could use something. Do you mind if we stop for a minute?"

"Not at all," Sage said. "Go ahead." They stopped at a café and MJ placed her order.

"Are you sure you don't want something? A water perhaps?"

Sage thought for a moment. "Sure, I'll have a water."

MJ handed Sage a bottle of water. "Who was leading?" she asked.

Sage thought for another moment, "We both did. You led us here and stopped and got me to ask for some water. Then you followed my request and bought me a bottle."

MJ smiled, took a sip of her drink, and started walking again.

Sage's mind was awash with this leadership/followership thing. They walked in silence for a short while. "How can someone usurp the authority of their supervisor?"

"It's only possible if they have a greater potential to influence," MJ responded. "That happens a lot in businesses and probably just as much in our profession. If Frank hadn't perceived me to have greater authority and influence, he would certainly have taken over the mediation. We would have ended in gridlock, or one side would have won and the other lost. There would have been no agreement because Frank wouldn't have allowed it."

"Okay, then it's also important to use the other person's perception of you to your advantage," Sage said.

"Absolutely," MJ said. "The three ships of success manifest themselves in a person's ability to get his or her point across and to accurately interpret what others are saying." MJ took another sip of her drink and brushed her hair to the side.

"It's starting to make sense," Sage continued, "when you put it all together. Communicating effectively requires listening with the intent to learn from and to understand the perspective of others. The only way to ensure a peaceful, consensual, and lasting resolution is through open, honest, and purposeful interactions. Do I have that right?"

"You do," MJ said. "Effective communication is critical. Every leader must decide how he or she wants an interaction to end. Good leaders know how to set clear, measurable goals and objectives, and they establish up front equal footing for the players involved. Trust is important too. Really, it's a prerequisite to achieving empathetic understanding. Level Three interactions are dependent upon trust. A lack of trust will inevitably lead to compromise at best but more likely to confrontation."

Sage nodded. "That's pretty profound."

"It wouldn't be of much value if it wasn't," MJ responded. "Good facilitators must have the ability to motivate people to exceed their own expectations because they themselves *want* and *choose* to, not because they *have* to. To get people to want to follow you, you need to use your abilities to influence and to be interpersonally dynamic."

"Followership?" Sage asked spontaneously. "Is that even a word? I don't think I've ever heard anyone use that term before."

"Of course it's a word," MJ said with a look of mock shock. "You don't think I'd make up a word, do you?" She smiled. "Wait," she said, "don't answer that. I just had a flash of someone we know doing a press conference." They both laughed.

"Followership," she continued, "is simply taking someone else's lead. Everything you and I have talked about since we started walking comes into play here. No one is likely to follow you if they don't trust you. At the same time, you can't lead if no one is willing to follow. But whether leading or following, you should do it with commitment. You must be willing to take direction and execute as instructed as in 'follow,' or be the first one in and the last one out in difficult times, that is, to 'lead.'

A good follower will be disciplined, dedicated, and avoid the urge to act on impulse. A good leader will put the needs of others first and always do that which is good and right. That's fairly simple, right?"

Sage nodded, "It seems to be, but then why do so many people do it so poorly?"

"Sometimes it's because they don't trust or respect each other," MJ said. "Sometimes it's because they don't understand what's required of them. At other times, it's because they just don't care."

"That's just wrong," Sage said.

"Sometimes it is," MJ agreed. "But even when everyone knows what to do, there will be those who refuse to follow. Some people know they're disagreeing without reason, but they do it anyway. Here's an example: I went to visit a friend. When I got there, he was discussing the merits of private citizens carrying concealed weapons with some guy I didn't know. My friend had a boat-load of facts and statistics to support his argument. The other guy, not so much. There came a point in the discussion when this guy said, 'I don't care what your statistics show, and I don't care if the facts you're quoting are correct. I want to believe what I believe, and that's that!' A classic Level One interaction. And the 'leadership/followership' thing didn't exist in this case. No leader, no follower, just rivals."

Sage looked at MJ, "It seems the very nature of Level One is to shun clarification. It's like people don't want to know. They just want to win. It doesn't matter if the other side is trying to understand them or not. Level One is Level One. The discussion can't evolve if either side hunkers down and refuses to budge."

"You're right," MJ said.

"I used to think that because I talked to people and got them to do what I wanted, I understood facilitation," Sage said. "I realize now that's roughly the equivalent of thinking that because I pass a bank on the way to work each day and occasionally make a deposit, I understand banking."

Sage was walking a little faster and MJ had to lengthen her stride to keep up. Sage kept walking and talking without noticing her companion's distress. "Level Three interactions require better thinking, active intelligent listening, and perhaps a bit more time. But I like the idea of making decisions based on information and empathetic understanding. I get that any decision could turn out the same as if I'd compromised. But now I'm beginning to recognize the difference between giving something up because I feel 'forced to,' and giving it because I 'want to.' When I give something up because it makes the best sense, I win. And if I can get people to follow my lead the way you do, everyone will be the better for it. I'll be a better leader if I follow your lead. I really like this stuff."

"MJ stopped dead in her tracks. It took Sage a few strides to notice. "Are we late for something?" MJ asked.

Sage looked puzzled. "I don't think so. Why?"

MJ let the breath rush from her lungs. "Because if we walk any faster, we'll be running."

Sage started laughing, bowed her head, and raised her hands as if she were about to pray. "I tend to do that when I get on a roll."

"Well, stop rolling," MJ said, laughing. "It's hard on my bunions!" Under her breath, but loud enough for Sage to hear, she said, "Should've worn my running shoes."

"I know you can lead," Sage said, smiling, "I was checking to see how well you could follow."

MJ began chuckling. Shaking her head, she walked to where Sage was standing. "I think I like leading better," she said. "It's easier to keep up." The two of them were grinning when they set off again.

"Now, where were we?" MJ asked. Sage started to answer but MJ cut her off. "Oh no you don't," she said with a wave of her hand. "I got this. I was going to talk about relationships. Yes, I think that's as good a place as any. Get to know the people you're going to be interacting with."

"Makes sense," Sage said.

"So, tell me what's the most important factor to building positive relationships."

"Good communication," Sage responded.

"Nice try, but no," MJ said.

"Commitment?" Sage asked.

"Another good attempt but…no."

"I give," Sage said, throwing her hands in the air.

"It's trust," MJ told her. "We just talked about that. Untrustworthy people aren't likely to generate much confidence. Your ability to influence others is based on their perception of your knowledge, position, charisma, and your ability to either reward them or punish them. The first four factors will enhance your propensity to be trusted. The more of these you possess or are perceived to possess, the greater the possibility others will trust you. The fifth however, punishment, is likely to instill distrust. If it's used judiciously, or perceived that way, it can also inspire trust. Unfortunately, people inclined to use coercion tend to alienate. They put others off. Force is indicative of confrontational thinking. The more coercive the interaction, the greater the possibility things will end badly."

"The five characteristics that are likely to engender trust," Sage said, "umm...perception of person's expertise, position or status, ability to punish," she rolled her eyes, "Charisma, and...what's number five again?"

"Ability to reward," MJ said, "but you seem to be stuck on charisma. Well... you can be rather charming at times, I suppose."

"Why thank you, MJ. How charming of you to say so!"

They both laughed.

Still chuckling, MJ started up again. "But like everything else in life, influence can be abused. Any form of influence that's misused will end in an outcome similar to punishment. If you're scornfully superior in the way you display your knowledge, your expertise will become a liability. The same is true of status. It might be okay in a monarchy, but Americans hate it when people try to lord it over them. The misuses of any trait will impair the credibility of the person using it. Take charisma, for example. You can tarnish your charisma by misusing any of the other forms of influence. And timing is everything so be smart when you're trying to be influential.

Sage looked around and spotted her car across the parking lot. "It seems we left the mediation only a few moments ago," she said. "When can we get together again?"

"For what?" MJ asked.

Sage looked surprised. "For me to pick your brain some more," she said. "I'm learning a lot and I'm eager to learn more."

"It's time for this little birdie to leave the nest," MJ said. "You can spend a lifetime learning, but the best teacher is experience. You need to put what you know into practice. I've enjoyed our time together, and I look forward to the times we'll share in the future. But for now, we're done."

Sage was momentarily speechless. She definitely was not 'done.'

"Farewell, Sage," MJ continued. "Wherever you fare, fare well." She smiled. "I've wanted to say that since I first read Tolkien."

Sage laughed and reached out for a hug. "I'll miss our talks," she said, holding MJ close and tightly.

"I'm only a phone call away," MJ said. "You're welcome

to call or stop by anytime." Sage let go of her hug and caught MJ's hand, squeezed it gently, then reluctantly let it go, too. Sage did an abrupt about face and walked toward her car. *Fare well*, she thought. *Fare well.*

Three Ships of Success

Leadership

The act of inspiring, motivating, influencing, or
managing the behaviors of others

Followership

Emulation of or exhibiting behaviors or actions
demonstrative of another's values or beliefs

Relationships

The involvement, connection, or association with
others whether positive or negative in nature

11

Conclusion

For those of you who might be wondering, Sage went back to her office and was very successful in applying what she'd learned. MJ's model for improving interpersonal interactions worked.

I use that very model every day, and it works for me, too. Admittedly, it's a different way of thinking. But if it were simply more of the same, it would be of no use.

There can be no progress in the absence of change. Our willingness to change, to be different, to stand apart from the norm is one of our greatest assets. On the contrary, one of the more debilitating issues of our time is our demand for assimilation and our desire to be just like everyone else.

When we readily accept the popular rhetoric of the day without question, without thinking it through, it hampers our ability to innovate and excel in endeavors that are outside the exploration of technology. Society is diminished when conforming is requisite to success. We impair our potential for greatness with our propensity to compromise.

It should be clear by now that compromise is a measure of mediocrity. Great people don't compromise, and that's a good thing. That's not to say that you shouldn't be thoughtful or introspective. News flash—not every idea you'll have will be a good one. It's important to continuously evaluate your thinking and, when faced with better information, to modify your position. I know that's not popular these days. Politicians are roundly and regularly criticized for adopting "new" positions. Watch any news channel, and you're likely to hear inane grousing about some politician who "flip-flopped." But it seems to me, when presented with information that no longer supports your position you *should* alter your thinking.

Being astute and adopting a new position is different than sacrificing for the sake of appeasement or compromising for the sake of getting along. Compromise is an avoidance behavior. Anyone can avoid making the tough decisions. It takes strength of character to find commonality. And once you've identified what you have in common there's no need to compromise. "Common" means "shared together." So look for the stuff you share, and reject the inclination to compromise.

Sage's story illustrates what most people believe about sacrificing and capitulating. Sage had a difficult time buying into that line of reasoning. From my perspective, the concept of compromise is a distraction that leads to settlements often having no relationship to the initial concern. Pork barrel politics are a classic example. Politicians slip incentives into bills that have nothing to do with the subject of the bill and call it a "compromise." A wife suggests taking an island vacation each year so that she and her husband can be alone. Her husband offers instead to take the family to the waterpark. Nice gesture, but it missed the point. Having an affinity for animals, a child asks to go to the zoo. Her mom offers instead to let her play with the neighbor's kitten. Such shenanigans are counterproductive to reconciling conflicting views or satisfying an actual need or desire.

In chapter four, Michael asked Sage which of her principles she was willing to compromise. It's a good question. *What are* you *willing to compromise?* Your right to peaceably assemble? Your right to own a firearm? How about your right to remain silent or to be free from unreasonable searches or seizures?

To get beyond compromise, we should admit the possibility that a lot of us aren't particularly articulate in the way we communicate. We all want to win. Of course, we do. Unfortunately, we've come to see everything as a contest of wills. Have you noticed how obsessed Americans are with fighting? The rhetoric of politics is to fight.

Social reformers are always "fighting" for something. The police *fight* crime, researchers *fight* cancer, medical professionals *fight* various diseases, the altruistic *fight* against poverty, and we're all fighting just to stay alive. But it doesn't stop there. We even fight when we're having fun. In football, we fight for yards. In basketball, we fight to the hoop, and we fight for the puck in hockey. We fight back tears or not to laugh. The list goes on.

Words have power. The way we describe a thing speaks volumes about how we're likely to approach it. What do you think would happen if we stopped "fighting" with our adversaries and started "working" with them?

Adversaries fight. Advocates work. If we work, we can all win. If we fight, only one of us will.

MJ pointed out the significance of identifying which level a person is coming from in their interactions. Level One brings conflict, ultimately leading to destruction. Level Two is also confrontational and the results are likely to be mediocre at best. For instance, the efforts to provide affordable health care for every American, or international efforts to mitigate the effects of global warming, or to improve multinational trade agreements are perfect examples of initiatives that have failed for decades. The solutions proffered until now have only further demonstrated the mediocrity of compromise. Aside from politics, even if you agree with the premise that carbon emissions have something to do with climate, the Paris Agreement was a mishmash. They set stiff targets to achieve, then backed off on all of them, and ultimately set up a way for emitters to buy their way out of it. The Affordable Care Act is a hodgepodge of pork.

Level Three rises above all of that. It offers the possibility for mutually satisfying outcomes. It can even lead to greatness.

People believe they have valid reasons to support the positions they accept as true. If you challenge their thinking, you can end up in a brawl. Conversely, people open to alternative views are sometimes seen as weak. That may or may not be true.

One thing is for sure. We all typically like to win. Sage told us right up front that she liked winning and prided herself on her ability to do so. She, however, had embraced compromise, believing it was the way for everybody to win. MJ showed her that compromise wasn't a win/win. Exposure to the Three Levels of Interaction opened Sage's eyes to a possibility for better outcomes.

It takes courage, patience, and commitment to work through the difficult machinations that lead to understanding, and to make decisions based on what's good and right.

It is true: Every war ends in one of three ways—annihilation, occupation or communication. If you consistently dominate your clients, employees, or the people you love, someone is going to lose. You're on Level One, which isn't where you want to be.

It is possible to annihilate a person and perhaps to even feel good about it, but to what end? You won't endear yourself to anyone you purposefully destroy. You may be one of those blessed with the ability to argue any position. Avoid that temptation. You'll only alienate your opponent and damage your chances for an empathetic understanding by turning a would-be advocate into an adversary. You're still on Level One.

People who avoid making the tough decisions tend to look for what they believe to be an easier way out. We've been told that compromise is a win/win, the preferred way to get things done. It isn't. Compromise is a highway to mediocrity. Everybody loses. No one leaves the experience satisfied or happy. The idea that anyone would agree to hours, days, weeks, months or even years of trying to find a solution to make everyone involved unhappy is the height of absurdity. The only way for everyone to win is to get off Level One, bypass Level Two, and move to Level Three.

The *Five Pillars of Level Three Interactions* are a foundation for the purposeful management of *any* interaction. Whether it's a corporate merger, a small business startup, or a family discussion, the process works: 1) Let people tell you their story, 2) Set mutually acceptable objectives, 3) Empower others, 4) Engage in Active Intelligent Listening, and 5) Provide an honorable way out for those who need it.

Interacting on the Third Level requires you to think differently. It's a paradigm shift that requires the use of Active Intelligent Listening to; 1) Seek out the motivations of others, 2) Separate fact from fiction and 3) Satisfy the actual needs of the people involved. Essentially, you experience life through the eyes of another with the intent of finding commonality through the synthesis of previously unshared experiences.

The *Three Ships of Success* allow you to assume the best posture for any interaction. The relationships you build are critical to your ability to work effectively with others. The level of influence you'll have is dependent upon how other people perceive you socially and/or professionally. Whether you're viewed as charismatic, an expert, having position or social status, having the ability to reward people or to punish them, or all of the above will invariably affect the nature of any relationships you'll ever have.

It doesn't matter whether you're leading or following. You need others to trust you. Sometimes the best way to lead is to follow. But either way it's important to note that you can't lead if no one will follow. And no one will follow anyone who isn't trustworthy. People need to know they can count on you.

The purpose of this book is to get you to interact with the intent of learning from and empathetically understanding the perspectives of others. Knowing which level your counterpart is on allows you to reframe the interaction to move to the Third Level. You may not always be successful, but that should be your goal.

Interacting on the Third Level is a way to peace. It is an eminently viable way to ensure responsive, responsible, and mutually satisfying results. Knowing there is a third level of interaction beyond confrontation or compromise can be empowering. If you live on the Third Level and honor the Three Ships—personally and professionally—you'll invariably improve your interpersonal interactions, your relationships, and ultimately your happiness.

Whatever your choice, make it your level best.

About the Author

Donald Grady, PhD, is a creative, innovative public-safety entrepreneur and reputed expert in designing and implementing public safety reforms domestically and in post-conflict environments. He's served as the Senior Police Advisor to the Minister of Interior in Iraq, Deputy Commissioner for Planning and Development in the United Nations Mission in Kosovo; the Senior Police Advisor to the Organization for Security and Cooperation in Europe (OSCE); the Senior Police Advisor to the Palestinian Authority Police; and as the Regional Commander for the United Nations International Police Task Force in Brcko, Bosnia-Herzegovina. Dr. Grady developed the multi-ethnic democratic police service for the Municipality of Brcko and the International Police

Observer unit for the Brcko Region. He was responsible for the development and implementation of the International Police reentry plan for the reintroduction of international police personnel in Kosovo. Additionally, Dr. Grady has undertaken operational readiness assessments of the Kenyan National Police and the National Police in the Democratic Republic of the Congo.

Donald Grady is the author of *The Injustice of Justice*, *The Absurdity of Compromise*, and a case study of "Resistance to Change in the Santa Fe Police Department." He has a Master of Science Degree in Management and a Ph.D. in Administration and Management. Dr. Grady has completed studies at the Federal Bureau of Investigation's (FBI) National Academy in Quantico, Virginia, and the University of Northwestern School of Police Staff and Command in Evanston, Illinois. He attended the United Nations Staff College in Turin, Italy and the Nordic/United Nations, Senior Management Seminar for United Nations peacekeepers, in Helsinki, Finland and New York City.

Dr. Grady has been Chief of Police and Public Safety for Northern Illinois University, the Chief of Police for the City of Santa Fe, Chief of Police for the University of New Mexico in Albuquerque, and Chief of Police for the City of Bloomer, Wisconsin.

Dr. Grady has appeared on several news networks including ABC and ABC's *Nightline*, CNN, CBS, NBC and has made numerous guest appearances for television and radio talk shows locally, nationally, and internationally. He's been featured in the *Wall Street Journal*, the *Albuquerque Journal*, the *Santa Fe New Mexican*, *Santa Fe Reporter*, and many other local newspapers. Dr. Grady has been a guest speaker for the National Organization for Black Law Enforcement Executives (NOBLE), The International Association of Chiefs of Police (IACP), the United States Department of State, several chapters of the Lions Club, the Kiwanis Club, Toastmasters, and dozens of universities, colleges, and sports arenas.

Dr. Grady served as a commissioned and non-commissioned officer in the United States Army and Reserves.

He's been certified as a police instructor, served as an adjunct professor, and continues to speak publicly as a guest lecturer.

Acknowledgments

I am unlikely to ever find the words to express my appreciation for those who have put up with me so faithfully throughout the years. Thank you seems a terribly inadequate expression for such profound dedication and commitment. However, nothing strikes me as more befitting than to say thank you from the depths of my soul.

I owe much to my forever love, Christine Joy Grady. You've stood with me and by me through the good and the not so good. Your willingness to confer and advise has been invaluable and greatly appreciated. You are a very special lady.

I offer my undying gratitude to three of my favorite people in the world: Karen Edwards, RaMon Holland, and Leon Ward. I'm indebted to each of you for dedicating your time and energy to help with this endeavor. Your insights and inspiration unquestionably improved this work.

Lastly, to the young people in my life. For me, you're the hope of the future. One of humankind's greatest failings is our inability to transcend self. Be your best for others, do your best for others, and give your best to others, then reap what you have sown. I always have and always will love you.

www.ingramcontent.com/pod-product-compliance
Lightning Source LLC
Chambersburg PA
CBHW031402180326
41458CB00043B/6574/J